A History of Western Tragedies and Accidents

Nina Wegner

Level 4
(2000-word)

IBC パブリッシング

はじめに

　ラダーシリーズは、「はしご（ladder）」を使って一歩一歩上を目指すように、学習者の実力に合わせ、無理なくステップアップできるよう開発された英文リーダーのシリーズです。

　リーディング力をつけるためには、繰り返したくさん読むこと、いわゆる「多読」がもっとも効果的な学習法であると言われています。多読では、「1. 速く 2. 訳さず英語のまま 3. なるべく辞書を使わず」に読むことが大切です。スピードを計るなど、速く読むよう心がけましょう（たとえば TOEIC® テストの音声スピードはおよそ 1 分間に 150 語です）。そして 1 語ずつ訳すのではなく、英語を英語のまま理解するくせをつけるようにします。こうして読み続けるうちに語感がついてきて、だんだんと英語が理解できるようになるのです。まずは、ラダーシリーズの中からあなたのレベルに合った本を選び、少しずつ英文に慣れ親しんでください。たくさんの本を手にとるうちに、英文書がすらすら読めるようになってくるはずです。

《本シリーズの特徴》

- 中学校レベルから中級者レベルまで5段階に分かれています。自分に合ったレベルからスタートしてください。
- クラシックから現代文学、ノンフィクション、ビジネスと幅広いジャンルを扱っています。あなたの興味に合わせてタイトルを選べます。
- 巻末のワードリストで、いつでもどこでも単語の意味を確認できます。レベル1、2では、文中の全ての単語が、レベル3以上は中学校レベル外の単語が掲載されています。
- カバーにヘッドホーンマークのついているタイトルは、オーディオ・サポートがあります。ウェブから購入／ダウンロードし、リスニング教材としても併用できます。

《使用語彙について》

レベル1：中学校で学習する単語約1000語

レベル2：レベル1の単語＋使用頻度の高い単語約300語

レベル3：レベル1の単語＋使用頻度の高い単語約600語

レベル4：レベル1の単語＋使用頻度の高い単語約1000語

レベル5：語彙制限なし

Contents

●読み始める前に●

本書で使われている用語です。わからない語は巻末のワードリストで確認しましょう。

- ☐ assassinate
- ☐ behead
- ☐ bury
- ☐ crime
- ☐ divorce
- ☐ execute
- ☐ murder
- ☐ nuclear
- ☐ radioactive
- ☐ revolution
- ☐ royal
- ☐ tragedy

【ストーリーの紹介】

1. The Battle of Tours
トゥール・ポワティエ間の戦い

かつてイベリア半島の一帯を支配したイスラム帝国のウマイヤ朝は、西暦732年、ついに現在のフランスに侵入した。当時のフランク王国が防衛しヨーロッパ世界はかろうじて守られた。中世のキリスト教社会を震撼させたこの戦いは、宗教の対立のほかに果たしてどのような意味をもつのだろうか。

2. The Plague Arrives in Europe
ペストのヨーロッパ上陸

2019年に発生した新型コロナウイルスはパンデミックを引き起こした。同様に、中世にはペストが大流行し、人々を恐怖に陥れるとともに、当時の封建制度を瓦解させヨーロッパ社会を変革した。感染症と人類との関係は、古代から現代まで、そしてこれからも続いてゆく長い闘いなのである。

3. The Wives of Henry VIII
ヘンリー8世の6人の妻たち

ヘンリー8世(1491-1547)は、テューダー朝のイングランド王で、生涯6人の后と結婚・離婚を繰り返した。離婚を認めないローマ法王と断絶し、英国国教会を立てたことで知られる。2人の妻を死刑にしたほか、自分に反対する家臣を処刑し、修道院を破壊するなど暴君であった。

4. Bloody Mary
血まみれのメアリー

メアリー1世（1516–1558）は、カクテル「ブラッディマリー」の由来となったイングランドの女王。熱心なカトリック教徒だったことから、父ヘンリー8世が立てた英国国教会につらなるプロテスタントを迫害し、女性や子供を含め300人以上を処刑した。そのことから「血まみれのメアリー」と呼ばれた。

5. The Beheading of Marie Antoinette
悲劇の王妃マリー・アントワネット

マリー・アントワネット（1755–1793）は、幼くして故郷を離れ、若くしてフランス王妃となった。ヴェルサイユ宮殿で華やかな生活を送っていたが、その後王制に対する民衆の不満が募り、フランス革命が勃発すると、裁判で斬首刑を言い渡される。無実を訴えるアントワネットだったが、最後はギロチン台に送られることとなった。

6. The Assassination of Abraham Lincoln
リンカーン大統領暗殺事件

第16代アメリカ合衆国大統領エイブラハム・リンカーン（1809–1865）は、米国史上初めて暗殺された大統領である。奴隷制度を認めなかったリンカーンは、国を二分した南北戦争を戦い、その戦争末期に南部連合の支持者によって暗殺された。奴隷解放の父として名高い彼は、なぜ、暗殺されなければならなかったのか。

7. The Elephant Man
エレファント・マン

ジョゼフ・メリック（Joseph Merrick 1862–1890）は、身体が変形・肥大する奇病に冒され、その異様な風貌のために、後見人にも仕事にも恵まれず、見世物小屋での職も失った。しかし、彼の最後のときは、少なくともベッドの上であった。劇化、映画化もされ脚光を浴びた彼の壮絶な人生はどんなものであったのか。

8. Jack the Ripper
切り裂きジャック

19世紀末、ビクトリア朝時代のロンドンで、娼婦ばかりを狙った残忍な殺人事件が連続発生する。当時のメディアを賑わせ、世間を震撼させた犯人は、劇場型犯罪の祖とよばれている。事件はいまだに解決されておらず、犠牲者の正確な人数、犯行の動機なども不明のままである。

9. The Titanic
豪華客船タイタニック

豪華客船タイタニックは、1912年4月、処女航海中に沈没し1500人以上もの犠牲者を出した。この悲劇的な船の名は、映画化により世界的に有名となった。映画に描かれたドラマチックなエピソードには事実とは異なるものがある。しかしいくつかは事実に基づくものである。

10. The Execution of the Romanov Family
根絶やしにされたロマノフ王家

ロマノフ朝最後のロシア皇帝であるニコライ2世（1868-1918）は、革命勢力の手に落ち、まだ十代であった子供たちをも含めた一家全員が処刑された。人知れず埋められた一家の遺体は長い間見つからなかったものもあり、いくつもの伝説を生んだという。

11. The Kidnapping of Charles Augustus Lindbergh, Jr.
リンドバーグ息子誘拐事件

チャールズ・オーガスタス・リンドバーグ（1902-1974）は史上初めて、大西洋単独無着陸飛行に成功したパイロットとして知られている。しかしここで語られるのは彼の飛行中の事故ではなく、彼の1歳の長男の誘拐事件についてである。身代金目当ての誘拐事件は、最悪の展開を迎えることとなる。

12. **Bonnie and Clyde**
ボニー＆クライド

ボニー・パーカー（1910-1934）とクライド・バロウ（1909-1934）は、世界恐慌時代のアメリカを荒らしまわった犯罪者のカップルである。仲間たちとともに犯罪を繰り返し、ありとあらゆる種類の犯罪に手を染めた。愛し合う危険な2人の人生は、あまりにも波乱に満ちたものだった。

13. **Edward VIII's Love**
エドワード8世の王冠を賭けた恋

イギリス王子、エドワード8世（1894-1972）は、奔放なアメリカ人の人妻ウォリスと恋に落ちる。やがて王になった彼は、ウォリスとの結婚を願うが、周囲からの強い反対にあい、愛と王冠を秤にかけることになる。王冠を賭けた恋として知られる、彼らの恋の行く末は……。

14. **Amelia Earhart's Last Flight**
消えたアメリア・イアハート

アメリア・イアハート（1897-1937）は女性として初の大西洋単独横断飛行を達成した飛行士である。飛行機に魅せられた彼女は、数々の記録を樹立してゆく。しかし、赤道上世界一周飛行の挑戦途中、彼女との交信は途絶えてしまう……。

15. **The Assassination of John F. Kennedy**
JFK暗殺の謎

ジョン・F・ケネディ（1917-1963）の白昼の暗殺事件は、合衆国のみならず、全世界に衝撃を与えた。第35代アメリカ合衆国大統領に43歳という若さで就任し、数々の仕事を成し遂げ、人気もあったケネディ。誰に、なぜ、暗殺されたのか。その謎は現在に至るまで様々な憶測をよび続けている。

16. **The Assassination of Martin Luther King, Jr.**
キング牧師の暗殺

キング牧師（1929-1968）は、公民権運動の指導者として人種差

別と戦い、反戦を訴え、そして凶弾に倒れた。彼が死の前日に行ったスピーチは、彼の早すぎる死を予感させる内容であった。

17. Apollo 13
奇跡の生還、アポロ13号

1970年、アポロ13号は地球を飛び立った2日後、深刻なトラブルに見舞われた。乗組員たちは、急きょ地球へ帰還することになる。乗組員の生命を脅かす結果となり、かつ月面調査の使命を果たせなかったアポロ13号ではあったが、数々の危機を鮮やかに切り抜けたこの事件は、「栄誉ある失敗」ともよばれている。

18. Three Mile Island
スリーマイル島原子力発電所事故

アメリカで起こった最悪の原子力事故といえばスリーマイル島でのものであるが、この事故による死者はなく、周辺住民の健康への影響もほとんど見られなかったという不幸中の幸いともいえる事故であった。しかしこの事故が世間に与えた衝撃と恐怖は甚大なものであったことは間違いない。

19. The Murder of John Lennon
ジョン・レノン殺害事件

世界中で人気を博したビートルズの解散から10年が経過してもなお愛され続けたジョン・レノン（1940-1980）。彼の殺害は世界中のファンに衝撃と悲しみをもたらした大事件であった。ジョン・レノンのクリエイティブな精神は誰に、何のために中絶されてしまったのか。

20. Chernobyl
チェルノブイリ原子力発電所事故

1986年に起きたチェルノブイリ原子力発電所の事故は、世界最悪の原子力事故であり、深刻な事故（レベル7）と分類された。被爆による死者が多数出たこと、その後の周辺住民への健康・生活へ与えた影響が計り知れない大規模災害となったことから全世界を震撼させてきた。

21. The Death of Princess Diana
悲劇のダイアナ妃

20歳でイギリス皇太子チャールズと結婚したダイアナ（1961-1997）は、若く美しきプリンセスとして世界中で「ダイアナ・フィーバー」を巻き起こした。それだけに、その後の不遇の結婚生活、そして離婚した後も、スクープを狙うパパラッチたちの格好の的であり続け、悲劇的な事故へと巻き込まれてしまう。

22. 9/11
アメリカ同時多発テロ

2001年9月11日に起きたアメリカ同時多発テロは、アメリカのみならず世界中に大きな衝撃を与えた。ハイジャックされた4機の飛行機が次々と高層ビルや政府機関の建物に激突・墜落。テロの犠牲となった大勢の人をはじめ、その後のアメリカによるイラクへの報復戦争においても、大勢の命が失われた。

23. Tesla Unveils the Model Y
テスラがモデルYを発表

2019年3月14日、電気自動車で業界のさきがけとなったテスラが、従来より電費を改善したモデルYを発表した。さらにAIによる完全な自動運転を目指し技術革新を続ける同社は、単なる自動車メーカーではなく、AIでの新分野を切り開くパイオニア企業だ。21世紀の産業界をリードするのはAIなのだ。

24. The U.S. Capitol Riot
アメリカ連邦議会議事堂乱入事件

2020年のアメリカ大統領選挙で、世界との協調路線を捨てたトランプ氏と右傾化に歯止めをかけたいバイデン氏とが真っ向から対決した。全米を二分した激戦を制したのはバイデン氏だったが、結果に不満を抱いた人々が大規模な抗議活動を展開。そして、2021年1月6日に、前代未聞の大事件が起こる。

A History of
Western Tragedies
and Accidents

1.

The Battle of Tours

If you look at the Spanish flag, you will notice that it has several emblems in its center. Let's look at the bottom one, which is a pomegranate fruit and leaf.

It is a symbol of the Islamic dynasty that ruled the southern part of Spain, and it tells us that most of Spain was controlled by Islamic kingdoms at one time. The state founded by Muhammad, the originator of Islam, was taken over by the Umayyad Empire in 661 A.D., and it expanded rapidly over the next 50 years. The Umayyads quickly expanded their power from North Africa in the west to what is now Afghanistan and Pakistan in the east, and then into the Iberian Peninsula to Europe.

In 732 A.D., the soldiers of the Umayyads finally invaded what is now France. The invasion of the Muslims across the Pyrenees Mountains on the border with Spain must have been a major event not only for France but also for the Christian world in the Middle Ages.

In the western part of France, between the cities of Tours and Poitiers, the Frankish ruler of the time, Charles Martel, knowing that he must somehow stop the invasion, was lying in wait for them. Charles Martel made good use of the terrain and forests in the area and utilized his infantry to distract his opponents. Records indicate that that Umayyad army was planning to bring France into its empire, and had brought not only soldiers but cattle, horses, and family members with them. The attack by infantry hidden in the forest was highly effective against such an army. In the end, Charles Martel's army was able to drive out the Muslim attackers, barely managing to save the Western world.

Around 732, Europe was halfway through the Middle Ages. It was a time when the Roman Catholic Church dominated as the spiritual pillar of Western Europe. In order to increase its authority, the Roman Catholic Church severely restricted any intellectual activities that might shake the foundations of its own religion. Even the exploration of science, which had been encouraged during the Greek and Roman eras, was persecuted as an obstacle to faith.

Although many things were lost in Europe, much of the civilization that had been nurtured in the Mediterranean world for many years prior to the Middle Ages was preserved and cultivated in the Islamic world. It is said that in those days, knowledge from all over the world was stored in books in the library in Baghdad. Against this backdrop, we can see that the Umayyads enjoyed a civilization far richer than that of Europe at the time.

Arthur C. Clarke, a well-known science fiction writer and expert on science, explained that if the Muslims had won the Battle of Tours, the Industrial Revolution and the subsequent history of modernization would likely have happened a thousand years earlier.

Some 700 years after the Battle of Tours, as the Pope's authority began to decline, a movement to reexamine the culture of past European civilizations sprung up, giving birth to what is known as the Renaissance. Clarke's theory, it seems, may be correct.

European Intellectuals of the Renaissance imported the cultures of such civilizations from the Islamic world. The Renaissance was a great revival of learning, but it would not have been possible without the texts that had been accumulated and preserved in the Islamic world.

On the other hand, in 1096, 364 years after the Battle of Tours, Europeans began to send crusaders into Muslim lands in a military campaign to retake the holy city of Jerusalem.

The start of the full-blown confrontation

between Christian and Islamic societies can be traced back to this point. In response to these developments, a movement began in Western Europe to drive Muslim society out of the Iberian Peninsula and establish a Christian state.

After years of fighting, the Muslim states on the Iberian Peninsula were finally destroyed in 1492. After that, Spain became one of Europe's most strongly Roman Catholic countries.

In order to maintain the country's financial resources, Spain sent many explorers, including Columbus, to the farthest reaches of the ocean. It was also in 1492 that Columbus traveled to the New World.

The Spanish flag is colored red and yellow, representing the red of the blood shed in the battle to exterminate the Muslims and conquer the new continent, and the yellow of the golden wealth gained from it. Certainly, the battles between Muslims and Christians were horrific. But at the same time, it is also true that, ironically, the European world imported a great amount of science and knowledge from the Islamic world because of these struggles. The scientific exploration after the Renaissance, which was nurtured and came to fruition through these activities, transformed Western society and brought about the prosperity that still exists in the present day.

As a matter of fact, people of Middle Eastern descent living in Europe and the U.S. today resent the fact that these things have been forgotten and that Western culture is assumed to be scientific while the Islamic world is thought of as barbaric. Their pride in their heritage, along with the Palestinian issue, which has become more confused with the subsequent appearance of Israel, has stirred up great anger in their hearts.

In fact, throughout the long history of the Middle Ages, it was the Islamic societies that were more tolerant of religious diversity. The Roman Catholic Church did not accept any infidels, and even within Christianity, sects that disagreed with them were persecuted as heretics.

In Islamic society, however, freedom of

religion was guaranteed as long as taxes were paid. This permissive policy was one reason for their prosperity. It is sad to note, however, that these facts have been forgotten, and the image of Islam as a stubborn religion that excludes other religions has taken root.

Both Islam and Christianity have their roots in the same monotheistic religion. In recent years, the turmoil in the Middle East has led to the emergence of Islamic fundamentalists who have engaged in radical terrorist activities, which in turn has led to prejudice against Islam in Christian societies.

However, we should not forget the fact that when it comes to terrorist activities in the United States, the FBI is concerned not just with Islamic groups, but Christian ones as well. It will take a long time for monotheistic religions to be able to respect each other's differences and live in harmony. Until such an ideal is achieved, the large number of immigrants from the Middle East coming to the West will continue to be frustrated by society's ignorance of their civilization.

The Battle of Tours will be passed down to future generations as a battle to protect the Roman Catholic Church, one of the foundations of Western society. After winning the battle, Charles Martel's position in the Frankish kingdom was secure, and his grandson, Charlemagne, became Charles the Great. He was given the crown of the Roman Empire as the protector of the Roman Catholic Church.

2.

The Plague Arrives in Europe

The outbreak of the SARS-CoV-2 virus in 2019 caused a pandemic the following year when it spread around the world. This had a huge impact on economic exchange and travel.

In 2021, vaccinations are becoming common, and although infections are gradually slowing, some experts believe that it will take several years for people's lives to return to the way they were before the spread of the infection. The COVID-19 pandemic, which has already infected more than 250 million people worldwide and killed more than 5.15 million, is the deadliest threat since the Spanish Flu of 1918, which lasted for two years.

Pandemics have a major impact on people's lifestyles. In the case of the COVID-19 pandemic, people were discouraged from eating out and commuting to the office, and traditional ways of working and socializing changed drastically. How this will affect our future is unknown at this point.

These current pandemics remind one of the impact that plague in the Middle Ages had on Western society. The plague, also known as the Black Death, causes internal bleeding and blackening of the skin when infected. The source of infection is small animals, especially rats, and it is believed that fleas and other animals that have drunk the blood of rats can infect people. Because of its high mortality rate, the plague was mankind's most feared and abhorred disease from ancient times until the 19th century. The pandemic that spread across Europe in the 14th century was the most devastating in the long battle between mankind and this sickness.

It was in China that the plague first raged. It is said to have begun around 1320. At that time, the Mongol empire was a superpower that dominated the Eurasian continent. The emergence of this great empire, which stretched from China to Eastern Europe, stimulated the flow of people, and the plague slowly spread westward. Finally, about 20 years later, a case of the plague appeared on the island of Sicily, near the southern tip of Italy. In the blink of an eye, the plague spread throughout Europe.

The mortality rate was high to begin with, and there was no cure, so nothing could stop it from wiping out villages and towns. Some experts say that the population of Europe was reduced to one-third of what it had been. Since the population before the plague was said to have been around 70 million, one can imagine how serious the pandemic was. This pandemic terrorized people for 70 years.

People at that time believed the plague was a punishment from God. This led to all sorts of false rumors and sometimes even persecution of non-Christians. In particular, there are records of massacres of Jews in various locations. In addition, quack remedies spread throughout the country, which led to further infections. There were even incidents where villages were burned to the ground after an outbreak.

Wealthy people left the unsanitary cities and fled to rural territories to live. Boccaccio's masterpiece, *The Decameron*, is known for its amusing depiction of such people.

On the other hand, even in rural areas, the peasant population, which was already suffering from poverty, decreased drastically, and the lords often had difficulty collecting taxes. Peasant revolts broke out frequently in the territories that forced them to pay. At the same time, Europe was in the midst of a series of wars over royal inheritance and territory, such as the Hundred Years War between England and France. Such wars likely contributed to the spread of the plague. These problems led to the population of both countries being reduced by half in a short period of time, and exhausted their entire societies.

As this vicious cycle repeated itself, the feudal lords found themselves in a difficult situation both economically and politically. As a result, the foundations of the feudal system itself, in which society was held together through the service of lords to their king, began to crumble. The plague was the beginning of a fundamental change in medieval society. The exhaustion of the lords led directly to the strengthening of the power of the kings. The kings of Europe wanted to be independent of the Pope, who was the leader of the European world in the Middle Ages. This contributed to the Reformation, which criticized the religious policies of the Roman Catholic Church.

In addition, the plague struck Europe many times in the following years, and people panicked each time. Every time this happened, desperate measures were taken in various places to somehow escape the disease. In 2007, a large cemetery where victims of the plague were buried was unearthed in Venice, Italy. It is considered to be a valuable resource that suggests that plague victims were gathered and buried on an island called Lazaretto Vecchio, a short distance from the city.

Speaking of the plague and Venice, here is another important fact. The word "quarantine," which is used today as a way to isolate people who may have an illness, originated from the plague control in Venice. During the pandemic of the 14th century, people were quarantined on ships for 40 days before they could enter the port of Venice. This is the origin of the word "*quarantena*." If the plague were to spread in a city surrounded by sea, it could cause the city to collapse. It is interesting that the idea of quarantine existed at a time when the facts about infectious diseases were still unknown.

The plague of the Middle Ages revolutionized European society and led to the Reformation and the Age of Discovery. That makes one wonder what kind of future the coronavirus pandemic will create. The relationship between infectious diseases and humankind is a long battle that has lasted from ancient times to the present, and will continue in the future.

3.

The Wives of Henry VIII

Henry VIII was the king of England from 1509 to 1547. Some say Henry VIII was one of the most interesting kings to have ever ruled England. However, he is perhaps best known for the terrible way he treated his six wives. As soon as he became tired or bored with one woman, he simply got rid of her and moved on to another woman. He even killed two of his wives. Today, there is a little poem that describes the sad fates of his wives:

King Henry the Eighth,
To six wives he was wedded.
One died, one survived,
Two divorced, two beheaded.

Catherine of Aragon was Henry VIII's first wife. She was a good wife and a popular queen among the people of England. However, try as she might, she could not give Henry a son. Her one child who survived was a girl, Mary. Henry wanted a son to become king after him, and he had begun an affair with a young lady named Anne Boleyn. In order to marry Anne, Henry separated with Catherine.

Anne and Henry's marriage lasted only a little less than three years. She was beautiful and clever, but like Catherine of Aragon, she could not produce a son. Soon, Henry became tired of her and came up with a plan to have her killed. Anne was charged with several crimes against the state and she was beheaded on May 19, 1536.

After Anne, Henry moved onto his third

wife, Jane Seymour. A year after their marriage, Jane gave birth to a healthy baby boy, Henry's first son. He was delighted, but Jane died just 12 days later, from health problems caused by labor.

Anne of Cleves was Henry's fourth wife. Their marriage lasted only six months before Henry arranged a separation. Then he married Catherine Howard, a woman from a noble family who was young and pretty. Their marriage only lasted one year. When Henry found out Catherine was having an affair with another man, he quickly had her beheaded too.

Henry's sixth and final wife was Catherine Parr, a woman who was married twice before. Her first two husbands had died, and so did Henry. She is the only one of Henry's wives who did not die or go through divorce. There are many stories, movies, and plays today about the life of Henry VIII and the lives of his six wives.

4.

Bloody Mary

Bloody Mary is the name that was given to Mary I, Queen of England and daughter of Henry VIII by his first wife, Catherine of Aragon. Mary was given this name because she cruelly killed hundreds of Protestants for their religious beliefs. Although Mary ruled over England for only five years, she killed over 300 people, and she threw others into prison.

Mary was born on February 18, 1516. While Mary was growing up, it was clear that her parents' marriage was failing. Henry wanted to divorce her mother, Catherine, because she was not producing him any sons. Catherine was sent away from the royal court and Mary was not allowed to visit her mother.

When Mary was 17 years old, Henry VIII married Anne Boleyn. To make this marriage legal, Henry broke from the Catholic Church because Catholicism did not allow him to separate from his first wife, Catherine. Henry then established his own religion, the Church of England, of which he named himself the highest leader. Because Catherine was no longer the wife of the king of England, that made Mary no longer a princess. Anne Boleyn gave birth to a baby girl, Elizabeth, and she became the next in line for the throne instead of Mary. This upset Mary so much that she stopped speaking to her father.

Henry's third wife, Jane Seymour, finally gave the king a son, who was named Edward. Jane also wanted peace between Henry and Mary. Father and daughter finally began to speak to each other again, and before Henry died, he made Mary a rightful heir to the throne again.

When Henry died, his son Edward became king, but he died at the age of 15 from illness. At this point, another relation of Henry VIII, Lady Jane Grey, became the next ruler of England, but Mary fought back. She believed nobody had the right to rule England but herself. Through some political moves, she had Lady Jane Grey beheaded, and Mary finally became Queen of England in 1553.

Although her father had angered the leaders of the Catholic Church, Mary herself was a devoted Catholic. She believed Roman Catholicism was the only true religion, and her leadership as the Queen of England created a time a terror for anyone in the country who was not Catholic. Over 800 well-known Protestants left England while Mary was queen to try to escape prison or death.

The people Mary executed were burned alive, but many also died in prison. It is believed that Mary died from cancer in 1558. Although more Protestants were killed or imprisoned after Mary's death, the religious policy of hunting and killing Protestants ended several years after her death.

Today, the idea of Bloody Mary has led to the creation of a popular ghost story. It is believed that if a person looks into a mirror at midnight and says the name "Bloody Mary" three times, she will appear in the mirror. Some say the ghost of Bloody Mary will kill the person who called her name. Others say Bloody Mary will tell the person his or her future.

5.

The Beheading of Marie Antoinette

The French Revolution was one of the bloodiest events in the history of France. Of all the famous historic figures to die in the French Revolution, Marie Antoinette, Queen of France, may be one of the most famous today.

Marie Antoinette was born on November 2, 1755, the daughter of Francis I, ruler of the Holy Roman Empire, and Maria Theresa, the Queen of Hungary and Bohemia. She grew up in her parents' royal court in Vienna, Austria, surrounded by her 14 brothers and sisters. When she was 15 years old, she was married

to Louis-Auguste, the Prince of France. Four years later, Louis became the King of France, and Marie Antoinette became the queen at only 19 years old.

At first, the people of France were charmed by Marie Antoinette's personality and beauty. But this slowly wore off over the years. First of all, Marie Antoinette's marriage to Louis XVI was full of difficulties. The royal court of France expected the new king and queen to produce children to carry on the royal line. However, even after seven years of marriage, Louis XVI and Marie Antoinette had no children. Rather than spend time with his wife, Louis XVI preferred to spend time on his favorite interests, such as hunting and making locks. Second, Marie Antoinette became famous for spending too much money. To fight the feeling of sadness and failure she experienced from having a husband who was not interested in her, she spent more and more money on clothes and gambling. This angered the French public. While the people of France went without eating because they were so poor, here was Marie Antoinette spending money on shoes, dresses, games, and jewels.

Finally, in 1778, Marie Antoinette had her first child. But the baby was a girl, not a boy, and a boy was needed to carry on the royal line. In 1781, she had another child, this time a boy, and he was named Louis Joseph Xavier François, the Prince of France. However, by this time, Marie Antoinette was very unpopular among the French people. The birth of a prince did not make the public happy. In 1785, Marie Antoinette gave birth to a second son, Louis Charles, and she had another daughter in 1786, but the baby died only a year later.

By 1789, the royal court was in ruins. Louis XVI had created many political failures, such as helping to pay for the American Revolution, which led to France running out of money.

The king's ministers always tried to pay for the court's mistakes by raising the people's taxes, which the people could not afford anymore. The people of France were sick and tired of paying for the king's mistakes. They decided it was time for a new government. The French Revolution began.

In 1789, Marie Antoinette's oldest son, Louis Joseph Xavier François, died. Despite her deep sadness, Marie Antoinette continued her duties as queen. During this time, new laws were written that limited the powers of the king. Many people of the royal court left France, fearing that they would be assassinated. The people of France forced the royal family out of the palace at Versailles, and Marie Antoinette could have left France with her children. But they stayed in France to support Louis XVI.

By 1792, it was clear that the French royalty had fallen. Louis XVI was put on trial for crimes against the French public. He was found guilty and was beheaded in 1793. It was only a matter of time until Marie Antoinette's life would end in the same way.

Several months after the death of her husband, Marie Antoinette was put on trial for crimes that were mostly untrue. However, she was found guilty and also sentenced to death.

On October 16, 1793, Marie Antoinette's hair was cut off, and she was driven through Paris in an open wagon. She wore only a simple white dress. She was taken to a town square where a crowd of hundreds of people had gathered to watch her die. As she got out of the cart, she stepped on a man's foot by accident. Her last words were, "Pardon me, sir, I did not mean to do it." She was then walked up to a stage where she was beheaded.

Her son, Louis Charles, died in prison two years later. Her daughter was returned to Austria. Although she married, she died without any children, leaving nobody left to carry Marie Antoinette and Louis XVI's family line.

6.

The Assassination of Abraham Lincoln

One of the United States' best-loved presidents, Abraham Lincoln, was also one of four presidents to be assassinated. Lincoln was the sixteenth president of the United States and is famous for ending slavery and ending the Civil War, a bloody war that threatened to break apart the United States. Lincoln also led great changes in the American economy and the role of the national government. But many people at the time, especially Southern men who did not support the outcome of the Civil War, did not like Lincoln's policies. One group of men led by the famous stage actor John Wilkes Booth planned the deaths of the president, the vice president, and the secretary of state so the Southern states could break from the American government.

On the morning of April 14, 1865, Abraham Lincoln was in an unusually good mood. He and his wife, Mary Todd Lincoln, had plans to watch the play *Our American Cousin* that night in Ford's Theatre. John Wilkes Booth, who was an actor at the theater, found out the president's plans for that evening and decided it would be the perfect opportunity for the assassination. He planned to shoot the president as he watched the play.

That night, there were about 1,700 people attending the play at Ford's Theatre. The Lincolns arrived late and entered the Presidential Box, the private seats reserved for the president. When the Lincolns arrived, the play was paused and the band played "Hail to the Chief." The crowd cheered loudly for their president. Then, at about 10:25 p.m., John Wilkes Booth arrived outside the Presidential Box. The guard, recognizing Booth as the famous actor, allowed Booth to enter the Presidential Box.

Booth, who knew *Our American Cousin* by heart, waited until the actor on stage said one of the funniest lines in the play. He hoped to use the crowd's laughter to cover the sound of his gun. Just as the crowd broke into laughter, Booth shot Lincoln in the back of the head.

It took several minutes for the people in the theater to realize what had happened. Booth escaped by running across the stage, making it look as if he was actually part of the play. It gave him several minutes to escape, but Mary Todd Lincoln's screams finally informed people that the president had been shot. The theater broke into madness.

Although there was a doctor in the theater who rushed to Lincoln's side, it was too late. Lincoln was still alive but wouldn't be for much longer. The wound was too serious for the president to survive. The doctor and several other men were able to carry the president out of the theater and into a hotel across the street, where they laid him on a bed. The president's top ministers rushed to the room, but Lincoln's wife was so overcome with grief that she had to be taken out of the room.

On the morning of April 15, 1865, at 7:22 a.m., Abraham Lincoln died. Millions of people witnessed his funeral procession as his body left Washington, D.C., and was taken to Springfield, Illinois, where he grew up. After a 10-day search for John Wilkes Booth, the U.S. military found him hiding at a farm in Virginia. Booth was shot and killed.

One interesting thing about Lincoln's death still puzzles people today: just three days before he was assassinated, Lincoln told his friends about a bad dream he had had. In the dream, he wandered all through the White House, hearing the sounds of people weeping. Finally, he entered a room where many people were gathered. They were all weeping. A dead body lay in the center of the room, guarded by soldiers.

"Who in the White House has died?" Lincoln asked in his dream.

"The president," said the soldiers. "He has been assassinated."

Three days after he had this dream, Abraham Lincoln became the first U.S. president to be assassinated.

7.

The Elephant Man

The life of Joseph Merrick, known to the world as the Elephant Man, was short and lonely. Merrick was born in Leicester, England, on August 5, 1862. To everyone who saw him, he looked like a healthy baby boy, and he stayed this way for the first few years of his life. However, nobody knew that Merrick had a disease that would not only change the course of his life, but also kill him.

The first signs that something was wrong with Merrick showed when he was five years old. Some of his skin was thick, lumpy, and gray. There was also swelling on his lips, and soon, a large bump formed on his forehead. As the years went on, his right arm grew much larger than his left, and both of his feet also swelled up. Although he was made fun of by classmates and rejected by many people, Merrick continued to go to school. His mother also loved him dearly and took good care of him. But in 1873, when Merrick was only 10 years old, his mother died. His father married another woman, who also had children from her first marriage. Merrick went to live with them, but his new family did not treat him well.

Like many other people at the time, Merrick left school when he was 13 years old. But he had no way to support himself because nobody would give him a job. His condition made his speech difficult to understand, and his appearance made many people afraid of him. His father was always angry with him, calling him useless. Finally, when Merrick was 15 years old, he decided to leave home.

For a while, Merrick tried to find work, but

he ended up on the streets. An uncle of Merrick's took pity on him and brought him into his own home. He tried to help, but only after a few years, he realized he did not have enough money to support Merrick as well as his own young children. Merrick had no choice but to enter a workhouse.

Workhouses were places where young people who had no parents or other support could go to live in exchange for their work. The living conditions in workhouses were usually very poor, and after several years, Merrick felt he could no longer live in such a place. He decided his only escape would be to join a show of "human curiosities," otherwise known as freak shows.

Freak shows had been very popular throughout the 1800s in Europe and America, but by the late 1880s, they were starting to be looked down upon as cruel institutions. However, Merrick was given a team of managers who named him "the Elephant Man." Merrick was taken on the road and shown to strangers who paid to see such human curiosities.

During this time, Merrick met a doctor named Frederick Treves, who had come to see him. Treves felt that there was a lot to be learned from Merrick's condition, and he asked Merrick to come to the London Hospital to be examined. Although Merrick agreed, he soon stopped coming because the experience of being examined was so unpleasant. After this, Merrick's managers sent him to work traveling with a show through Europe.

However, freak shows were just as unpopular in Europe as they were in England. The traveling show did not do well. Merrick's manager at the time stole Merrick's life savings and left him alone in Brussels. Without money, a job, or any friends, Merrick returned to England.

But once he was back in England, Merrick had no home or friends who could help. His speech was so difficult to understand that when he asked strangers for help, they usually ran away. Finally, a police officer found him sitting on a street corner, surrounded by a crowd of curious people. He took Merrick to the police station and found that Merrick was carrying Frederick Treves's calling card. They called Treves, who came immediately and brought Merrick to London Hospital.

Once at the hospital, Merrick was given proper care. His health had become worse and worse over the past few years, but with good rest and food, Merrick gained back some of his health.

Treves knew that Merrick had nowhere else to go. He asked the chairman of the hospital to let Merrick live at the hospital, but the hospital did not have the money to support such an idea. The chairman wrote to local newspapers about Merrick's case. Merrick's story moved many readers and they sent the hospital money to keep Merrick there. Finally, it was decided that London Hospital would be Merrick's new home.

Merrick lived at the hospital for four years before he died. During these four years, his story became rather famous among London society, and some high-positioned families did what they could to help him. He was taken on several holidays to the country, he was brought to the theater to see a Christmas show, and he even received a visit from the Prince and Princess of Wales. Merrick spent much of his time reading and making models of buildings out of card paper. He seemed as happy as such a person in his condition could be.

Then, on the afternoon of April 11, 1890, Merrick was discovered dead, lying down in his bed. All his life, Merrick had had to sleep sitting up, resting his head on his knees, because his head was too heavy for his neck to support. He often told Treves that he wished to sleep lying down "like other people." When Treves saw his friend dead in bed, he believed Merrick had tried to sleep lying down. The cause of death was suffocation, caused by the weight of Merrick's head.

Today, there is a small museum in London dedicated to Merrick's life. And yet, nobody has ever figured out what Merrick's condition was.

8.

Jack the Ripper

"Jack the Ripper" is the name given to a serial killer who is thought to have murdered many people in the Whitechapel area of London in 1888. The murderer is also known as "the Whitechapel Murderer" and "Leather Apron." Although British police worked on solving the murders for years, the true murderer was never discovered. Today Jack the Ripper has become the subject of much research, movies, and popular fiction.

Although the murderer was never caught, the facts are still well known. In the late 1800s, the Whitechapel area of London was becoming crowded with many immigrants who had come to England looking for opportunities or a new start in life. Many of these people had no jobs and were very poor, and many women became prostitutes as a way to earn a living. Whitechapel came to be known as a low-class area of London, and after eleven murders were committed there between the years of 1888 and 1891, Whitechapel came to be known as a dangerous area too.

Out of the eleven murders that occurred during those four years, five are commonly thought to be the work of Jack the Ripper. According to police reports, Jack the Ripper had a set pattern in the way he operated. He only killed prostitutes. He always killed on the weekend, at night. He always killed each person first by cutting the throat, then he mutilated the body, especially in the region of the stomach. Sometimes the victim's face would also be mutilated and their internal organs would be missing. There were five Whitechapel murders that occurred close together in location and time that fit Jack the Ripper's pattern. These murders happened between the dates of Friday, August 31, 1888, and Friday, November 9, 1888.

Six other murders occurred around the Whitechapel area, but they did not fit Jack the Ripper's pattern. This has led some to believe that these others murders were not committed by Ripper, while others believe they were all his doing.

The news media at the time jumped on the story of a serial killer. They published stories that shocked the public and filled readers with terror. Newspapers sold like never before, and money flowed into the newspaper companies. Reporters were under pressure to keep telling the story of the murders in different ways so that newspapers would continue to sell. Sometimes this led reporters to make up details about the investigation, leading to deep confusion among the public and the police about what was true and what wasn't.

There were over 100 named suspects, but the police never caught the real killer. Who Jack the Ripper really was remains a mystery today.

9.

The Titanic

One hundred years after it sank, RMS Titanic is still one of the most famous ships in the world. The sinking of the Titanic is considered one of the worst Western sea accidents of all time.

The Titanic was built and designed by Thomas Andrews in Belfast, Northern Ireland. It took three years to build the Titanic, and it was to be the largest and grandest cruise ship in the world at the time. The Titanic was the second of three ships that were built for the White Star Line. The ship had the best facilities of any cruise ship at the time, including a gym, multiple libraries, a swimming pool, restaurants, and beautiful, private rooms for the passengers.

On April 10, 1912, the Titanic set sail on her "maiden voyage" from Southampton, England. The ship was bound for New York City. When the ship left the dock, there was great celebration, and all the media at the time were there. It was major news for the largest ship in the world to set sail on its first voyage. Waving goodbye to all the people gathered at the dock, the people aboard the Titanic were excited to begin their voyage. They felt that they were making history.

There were 2,224 people sailing on the Titanic. Some of the passengers were the richest people in the world, yet there were some of the poorest people too. These people without any money were trying to reach New York, where they hoped to get jobs and start a new life in America, a country that promised opportunity for all.

Before heading west to New York, the Titanic made two stops. The first stop was in Cherbourg, France, and the second stop was at Cobh, Ireland. After making these calls in port, the ship finally began to cross the Atlantic, heading for the final destination.

But on the evening of April 14, 1912, something went seriously wrong. It was 11.40 p.m., and the ship was about 600 kilometers south of Newfoundland when a terrible shock like an earthquake ran through the ship. The Titanic had hit an iceberg.

The iceberg bent and broke the bottom of the ship on the right side, causing five out of sixteen water-tight areas to flood. As the ship took on more water, the crew realized this was truly an emergency situation. They began to load passengers into lifeboats. However, the Titanic was not built with enough lifeboats to accommodate all the people onboard. There were only enough boats to carry 1,178 people. Many of the men stayed on the ship, letting women and children go first. As the boats were being loaded, some passengers decided to stay with their loved ones on the ship.

Only two and a half hours after the ship hit the iceberg, at 2:20 a.m., the Titanic broke apart and sank, with more than one thousand people still on the ship. As the ship was sinking, the band continued to play music.

Within two hours of the Titanic's sinking, another English ship, the Carpathia, arrived and saved about 710 people. But in total, 1,502 people died from the Titanic.

The sinking of the Titanic caused shock and anger around the world. People could not believe that such an accident could happen, leading to the death of over 1,500 people. This lead to the creation of many new rules and regulations for ship safety. The safety rules that came out of the Titanic accident are still followed today. The ship itself remains on the sea floor, broken into two pieces.

When the movie *Titanic* came out in 1997, it became an instant box office hit. It won the Academy Award for Best Picture, showing that the tragic and romantic story of the Titanic still speaks to the hearts of people today, more than 100 years after the accident.

10.

The Execution of the Romanov Family

The Russian Revolution of 1917 overthrew Tsarist rule and established a new government in Russia. This led to the Russian Civil War, which killed many people. Along with many soldiers who died fighting, many wealthy families were also put to death because of their wealth and privilege. The most privileged family of all, the Romanovs, was cruelly executed by the Red Army in 1918.

The Romanovs, consisting of Tsar Nicholas II, his wife Tsarina Alexandra, and their five children, were Russia's royal family. During the 1917 revolution, Tsar Nicholas II was overthrown and the Romanov family was imprisoned in their house. They lived as prisoners, watched by guards, until May 1918 when the family was moved to Yekaterinburg, an important military station of the Red Army.

In July 1918, the Red Army became afraid that Yekaterinburg would fall to the White Army, which was on the side of the royal family. This was a dangerous position for the Red Army. If the White Army freed the royal family, the tsar could get help from other European nations, who saw Tsar Nicholas as the true leader of the country. Under pressure to act quickly, the Red Army saw that there was only one thing to do: kill all the Romanovs at once.

The tsar's children were still very young at the time of their deaths. His four daughters, Olga, Tatiana, Mary, and Anastasia, were 22, 20, 19, and 17 years old, in that order. His son, Alexei, was the youngest at 13 years old.

In the early morning of July 17, 1918, the tsar's family and some of their helpers were awoken and told to get dressed. They were told that they were being moved to another house. After they put their clothes on, they were ordered into a small room. Once in the small, cold room, the family waited for what they thought would be a truck to pick them up. Instead, a top soldier of the Red Army walked into the room and announced that the new government had decided to execute the family.

Nicholas couldn't believe it and he reacted by asking, "What?" The soldier quickly repeated himself, then raised his gun and shot Nicholas in the head. The soldiers behind him immediately began to fire. The entire family and their few helpers were either shot or stabbed to death that night. Their bodies were buried at a secret site.

In 1991, the Russian government found five of the bodies and gave the royal family a proper funeral. The family was buried in Peter and Paul Cathedral in St. Petersburg. However, for a long time, two of the bodies—that of Anastasia and Mary—were missing. This led to many stories that Anastasia had survived the mass killing and had lived her life in secret. However, these popular stories were shown to be untrue when the missing two bodies were discovered in 2008.

11.

The Kidnapping of Charles Augustus Lindbergh, Jr.

Charles Lindbergh, the American pilot, was the first man to fly across the Atlantic Ocean by himself. Although he was famous around the world for a successful flying career, there was a great tragedy in his life. His two-year-old son was kidnapped and found dead several months later.

In the year 1932, many people in America were starting to feel the effects of the Great

Depression, but Charles Lindbergh was living his life as a happy husband and father in New Jersey. His son, Charles Augustus Lindbergh, Jr., was a healthy, beautiful baby. Life couldn't be better for the Lindberghs.

Then, on the night of March 1, 1932, Lindbergh's life changed forever. It was a normal night, and Lindbergh was relaxing in the library of his house. Betty Gow, the baby's nurse, had put the baby to sleep in his crib at around 8 p.m. Everything seemed normal, but at 9:30 p.m., Lindbergh heard a loud noise that sounded like a box of oranges in the kitchen breaking and falling.

At around 10 p.m., Betty went to check on the baby and discovered that the baby wasn't there. She asked Mrs. Lindbergh, who had just gotten out of the bath, if she had her son with her. When she said no, Betty went to ask Mr. Lindbergh. He wasn't with the baby either.

Lindbergh immediately went upstairs to the baby's room to see for himself. As he searched the baby's room, he found an envelope on the windowsill. The note contained a letter that demanded $50,000 and warned Lindbergh not to contact the police. It was clear then that the baby had been kidnapped and whoever had done it wanted a ransom.

Lindbergh ran outside with his gun and searched the grounds of the house, but he found no one. Twenty minutes later, the police arrived and began an investigation that was to go on for the next two years.

During the investigation, Lindbergh was so afraid that the work of the police would threaten the life of his son that he started his own private investigation. Helped by a man named John Condon from the Bronx, in New York, Lindbergh tried to contact the kidnappers to tell them he was ready to pay the money.

By placing personal ads in New York newspapers with a message to the kidnappers, Condon was able to set up a meeting with a man who claimed to be one of the kidnappers. The meeting occurred late at night at a local cemetery. Condon was told to come alone. He did, and he talked with a man who stayed in the shadows. The kidnapper said he was working with a group of people and that the baby was safe, but that the group was not ready to receive the money. Condon asked for proof that they had the baby and the man said he would mail the baby's pajamas as proof.

Condon received a package in the mail. It was the baby's pajamas. Roughly two weeks later, on April 1, 1932, Condon received a letter that said the kidnappers were ready for payment.

Condon and Lindbergh followed the kidnappers' instructions for a meeting and ended up at another cemetery, where they handed over the money. The money was put in a specially made wooden box so that it could be identified later. They also recorded the serial numbers of the dollar bills in the box so they could be tracked.

When Condon handed over the box of money, he was given a note that said the baby was being held on a boat called the Nelly in Martha's Vineyard in the state of

Massachusetts. Lindbergh immediately went to Martha's Vineyard but there was no boat called the Nelly. Almost crazy with grief, Lindbergh flew an airplane low over the boats to try to force the kidnappers out of their hiding spot, but no one came out. Lindbergh was crushed.

Roughly a month later, a truck driver stopped on his route to go to the bathroom on the side of the road. He was about 7 kilometers from Lindbergh's home in New Jersey. There, on the ground, he found the body of a baby. He called the police. The police contacted the Lindbergh family. The baby was wearing a shirt that his nurse, Betty Gow, had made for him. It was Lindbergh's son.

Two years later, the police finally found a suspect. By tracking the dollar bills included in the ransom money, the police were able to find Bruno Richard Hauptmann, a German immigrant with a criminal record. He was living in the Bronx in New York. When the police searched his house, they found John Condon's address and phone number written on his closet wall, among other evidence. Hauptmann was tried and found guilty. He was executed by electric chair on April 3, 1936.

12.

Bonnie and Clyde

Bonnie and Clyde are often thought of as the Romeo and Juliet of the criminal world. They were a very young, very dangerous couple living in America during the Great Depression. The couple and their friends were responsible for a dozen bank robberies, numerous murders, and at least a hundred other crimes and robberies. Bonnie and Clyde were truly in love, but they spent their short lives running from the law and were finally shot and killed by police.

Bonnie Parker and Clyde Barrow met in 1930 in West Dallas, Texas. Clyde was already a small-time criminal, stealing cars, opening safes, and robbing stores. Bonnie was married to a man named Roy Thornton, but they did not get long well, and they had separated. When Bonnie met Clyde, she was staying with a friend. Clyde stopped by the friend's house while Bonnie was in the kitchen making hot chocolate. When they met, it was love at first sight. Bonnie was 19 and Clyde was 21 at the time.

That same year, Clyde was sent to Eastham Prison in Texas, and he was not set free until February 1932. Prison was a very dark time in Clyde's life. He beat a man to death in prison. It was his first murder. His friends and family said he came out of prison as a different person—he had become a hardened criminal. He also came out with an impossible goal: to get his revenge on the Texas justice system for how it had treated him. Once he collected enough money and guns, he planned to attack Eastham Prison and set the prisoners free.

When Clyde got out of prison, Bonnie joined

up with him immediately. They formed a little group of friends and they traveled through the country, committing crime after crime. They mostly robbed banks and stores. The men often killed anybody who got in their way, although it was unlikely that Bonnie ever killed anyone. But as the nation became more and more aware of the group's many crimes, it became harder and harder for them to live. The police were after them in every city, and it was dangerous to go into hotels and restaurants. The group had to live mostly in hiding. After spending about two years on the road, the situation could not get much worse. A car accident also injured Bonnie's right leg and made it difficult for her to walk.

Bonnie and Clyde's short lives came to an end on May 23, 1934, in Louisiana. A group of police officers led by Texas Ranger Frank Hamer set up a surprise attack on a country road. They knew the couple would be driving down the road that day. The plan was to shoot them down as they approached.

At around 9:15 a.m., four police officers hid in the bushes along the road. As the car approached, the police officers recognized Clyde Barrow as the driver, with Bonnie Parker sitting next to him. They shot Clyde first and then Bonnie, and they continued to shoot until the car drove off the road. The police shot a total of about 130 rounds. The young couple was dead.

Bonnie and Clyde had wished to be buried next to each other, but Bonnie's family would not allow it. In the end, Bonnie was buried at Fishtrap Cemetery in Dallas on May 26, 1934. Clyde was buried next to his brother, Marvin, in Western Heights Cemetery in Dallas. The words on Clyde and Marvin's grave says, "Gone but not forgotten."

13.

Edward VIII's Love

Edward VIII was the only King of England who willingly gave up the throne. He gave it up after only a year of being king for a woman he had fallen madly in love with. The royal family and his ministers did not like his lover and would not allow him to marry her. The king then chose his lover over his role as king.

Edward VIII became king in January of 1936 when his father, George V, died. By this time, Edward had already been spending a lot of time with Wallis Simpson, a young, married American woman. At the time, Wallis had been married twice—she had divorced her first husband, married again, and was on her way to divorce her second husband.

Wallis was certainly not popular among Edward's relations, ministers, or even among many people in the general public. She was known in both British and American society as someone who was only interested in money, high positions, and social climbing. Edward's family thought Wallis did not act like a queen.

There were also political and religious reasons why Edward could not marry Wallis. As the King of England, Edward was the highest leader of the Church of England. The Church of England did not allow divorce, so the leader certainly could not marry someone who was divorced. Politically, Edward's ministers did not want him to marry Wallis because she was an American. At the time, the relationship between England and the U.S. was strained. England looked down on America as a lower-class nation, and the king's ministers told the king that the people of the British Empire would not want an American as their queen.

However, Edward was truly in love with Wallis, and he did have his share of supporters in government and in the public. He made it clear to his family and ministers that he would marry her. The only thing stopping him was that Wallis had not yet divorced her second husband.

In October of 1936, Wallis filed for divorce from her second husband. The news was made public, and everybody knew then that there was nothing stopping the king. On November 13, one of Edward's top ministers wrote to him, saying the marriage could only end in disaster. But just three days later, on November 16, the king told the British prime minister in a meeting that he intended to marry Simpson. He too, told the king not to do it. On December 5, having thought about all possible other options, Edward made his decision. He wrote his official notice that he would give up the throne.

On December 11, Edward was no longer king of England. His brother, Albert, was declared the new king. Edward ruled the empire for 327 days, which is the shortest rule any king or queen of England, except for Lady Jane Grey, has ever had. In May of 1937, Wallis's divorce went through, and in June 1937, Edward and Wallis were married. The marriage to the former king proved to be Wallis's third and final marriage: the couple stayed together for 35 years, until Edward's death.

14.

Amelia Earhart's Last Flight

In 1932, Amelia Earhart became the first woman pilot to fly by herself across the Atlantic. She made history with this flight and broke many other records in flying. However, while attempting to set a record as the first woman to fly around the world, Earhart disappeared into thin air. Nobody ever found out what happened to Earhart or her airplane.

Amelia Earhart was born in Kansas on July 24, 1897. She had one little sister, Grace Muriel Earhart, who was two years younger than her. The two girls grew up with a lot more

freedom than most girls at the time were allowed because their mother was a modern thinker who did not want to limit her children just because they were girls.

Earhart grew up playing outside with her sister, running through fields, climbing trees, and doing things that boys usually did. But as she was becoming a young woman, World War I broke out. Earhart got training at the Red Cross and began to work as a nurse at a military hospital. Although she helped many soldiers, she became ill with the Spanish Flu, which broke out in 1918. She was so ill that it took her about a year to recover. After she recovered, Earhart decided to go to college and entered Columbia University with plans to study medicine. But a year later, she quit school and joined her parents in California.

On December 28, 1920, Earhart's life

changed forever. That day, she and her father visited an airfield for fun. A pilot was giving people rides, and Earhart's father paid $10 for the pilot to take his daughter on a 10-minute ride. By the time Earhart landed on solid ground again, she knew that this was what she wanted to do with her life. She had to fly.

Earhart worked at all kinds of odd jobs to save $1,000, just enough money to take flying lessons with Anita Snook, a well-known female pilot. On January 3, 1921, Amelia Earhart had her first flying lesson, and six months later, she bought her own airplane.

On October 22, 1922, Amelia Earhart flew her plane up to a height of 4,300 meters, setting a world record for female pilots. On May 15, 1923, Earhart was given an official pilot's license. She was only the sixteenth woman in the world to receive one.

After Charles Lindbergh became the first man to fly by himself across the Atlantic Ocean in 1927, Amelia Earhart became the first woman to fly across the Atlantic in 1928.

She was accompanied by pilots Wilmer Stultz and Louis Gordon. However, she broke an even more important record in 1932 when she became the first woman to fly across the Atlantic by herself, with nobody else's help.

As Earhart's flying career became more and more successful, Earhart became one of the nation's most famous women. She was asked to be an editor at Cosmopolitan magazine, and she created her own clothing line. She married the American publisher GP Putnam, and she became one of the most respected American women of the time.

In 1936, Earhart began planning her most daring attempt of all: to fly around the world. Although it was not the first time that someone had attempted this, Earhart planned a path that was the longest ever attempted. She had a special airplane built with a large gas tank. She chose Captain Harry Manning and Fred Noonan to be her co-pilots.

The three-person team took its first attempt at flying around the world on March 17, 1937.

Earhart flew out of California and landed in Hawaii. However, the plane was damaged in Hawaii and the rest of the flight had to be canceled for plane repairs.

Earhart made her second attempt soon after, on June 1, 1937. This time, only Noonan went with Earhart, and they flew out of Miami, Florida, and made stops in South America, Africa, and Asia. The pair arrived in Lae, New Guinea, on June 29, 1937. They had completed about 35,000 kilometers of travel, and only had about 11,000 kilometers left. The rest of the trip would be over the Pacific Ocean.

Earhart and Noonan left Lae at midnight on July 2, 1937, with plans to land next on Howland Island, a small, flat, narrow island in the Pacific Ocean. The U.S. Coast Guard ship Itasca was stationed at the island to help communicate with Earhart over radio for her landing.

At 7:42 a.m. on July 2, the Itasca received a radio message from Earhart saying, "We must be on you, but cannot see you—but gas is running low. Have been unable to reach you by radio. We are flying at 1,000 feet." Another radio message came in at 7:58 a.m., saying that Earhart could not hear the Itasca. She asked them to send voice signals. The Itasca tried sending voice signals as well as Morse code. Earhart radioed back saying she got these signals but that she couldn't find the ship's location. In Earhart's last known message, she radioed the Itasca reporting her location. She said she would radio again, but another message never came.

Over the next few hours, the Itasca tried over and over to reach Earhart, but there was no clear answer. Soon, there was a full-on search for Earhart and Noonan on and all around Howland Island. The U.S. Navy also helped with the search. Within the next week, there were searches of the nearby Phoenix Islands. The official search lasted almost three weeks and cost about $4 million. But no sign of the two pilots or the airplane were found. Earhart and Noonan had simply disappeared.

After the official search ended, Earhart's husband, GP Putnam, conducted his own searches. But finally, after two years of searching, Amelia Earhart was declared dead on January 5, 1939. Although there are many guesses as to what happened to Amelia Earhart, today nobody knows. Searches for Earhart's airplane in the Pacific Islands continue. In May 2013, The International Group for Historic Aircraft Recovery announced that they discovered a 32-foot long object near the Phoenix Islands that could possibly be Earhart's plane.

15.

The Assassination of John F. Kennedy

John Fitzgerald Kennedy was the 35th president of the United States of America. He was the youngest president ever, and he was very popular and well-loved among the American people for his bright new ideas. He was shot and killed in the third year of his term as president, causing shock and grief across the nation and the world.

On November 22, 1963, President Kennedy

was traveling in an open-top car in a procession through downtown Dallas, Texas. He was in Dallas to attend a lunch meeting with some of the city's top leaders and businessmen. He had arrived at Dallas Love Field airport that morning, and he was going to drive through town in an open-top car to greet the people of Dallas on his way to the lunch.

It was a sunny day, and the procession was running about 10 minutes late. President Kennedy's wife, Jacqueline Kennedy, was sitting next to the president in the back seat of the car. Sitting in the front seat were Texas Governor John Connally and the governor's wife, Nellie Connally. Crowds had gathered all along the path of the procession with people who were excited at the chance to see the president. At around 12:30 p.m., the presidential car passed a building known as the Texas Schoolbook Depository near Dealey Plaza. Just at this moment, as the president waved to the crowds who lined the streets, he was shot once in his upper back and once in the back of his head.

Governor Connally was also shot in the shoulder, and after being shot, he cried out, "Oh no, no, no. My God. They're going to kill us all!" Special Agent Clint Hill, who was following the president in the car directly behind him, jumped into the president's car and tried to protect him. As soon as he jumped in, the car sped up and headed straight to Parkland Memorial Hospital.

The doctors who received President Kennedy at the hospital said Kennedy's condition was so bad when he arrived that he did not have any chance at survival. They tried all they could, but the president was declared dead at 1:00 p.m.

The body of John F. Kennedy was flown back to Washington, D.C., on Air Force One. Vice President Lyndon B. Johnson officially became the President of the United States on the airplane at 2:38 p.m. Kennedy's wife, Jacqueline, stood by Johnson's side.

John F. Kennedy's death caused the shock and grief of an entire nation. His body lay in state in the U.S. Capitol where hundreds of thousands of people came to pay their respects. Representatives from 90 countries attended the funeral on Monday, November 25. Kennedy was finally buried at Arlington National Cemetery in Virginia.

In the following ten months, a special team called the Warren Commission was ordered by the U.S. government to find out what happened. The Warren Commission was successful in finding a main suspect, Lee Harvey Oswald. He was tried in court and found guilty of the crime, but many people today believe that Oswald was not guilty. Today, many believe that the assassination, Lee Harvey Oswald, and the Warren Commission were all part of a government plan to assassinate the president, but nobody knows the truth.

16.

The Assassination of Martin Luther King, Jr.

Martin Luther King, Jr., was one of America's most important civil rights leaders. An African-American preacher from Macon, Alabama, King devoted his whole life to fighting racism in the United States. He won the Nobel Peace Prize in 1964 for his work. His efforts went a long way in winning equal rights for his fellow African-Americans, but he died fighting for these rights.

King died in Memphis, Tennessee, on the

night of Thursday, April 4, 1968. He had arrived in Memphis the day before to give a speech at a church event. It became the last speech he ever gave, and it is known today as the "I've Been to the Mountaintop" speech. Many have since pointed out the interesting fact that in this speech, King talked about his own death and the possibility that he might not live much longer. In the speech, he said:

"What would happen to me from some of our sick white brothers? Well, I don't know what will happen now. We've got some difficult days ahead. But it doesn't matter with me now. Because I've been to the mountaintop. And I don't mind. Like anybody, I would like to live a long life. Longevity has its place. But I'm not concerned about that now. I just want to do God's will. And He's allowed me to go up to the mountain. And I've looked over. And I've seen the promised land. I may not get there with you. But I want you to know tonight, that we, as a people, will get to the promised land! And so I'm happy, tonight. I'm not worried about anything. I'm not fearing any man. Mine eyes have seen the glory of the coming of the Lord!"

King would die the very next day.

On the night of April 4, King was staying at the Lorraine Motel, a hotel that he often stayed at when he was traveling in Memphis. He was booked in room 306, the same room he always stayed in at the Lorraine. That evening he was sharing the room with his friend and fellow civil rights leader, Ralph David Abernathy. Also staying at the hotel was musician Ben Branch. King's last words were to Branch, who was going to play music at an event King was attending that night.

"Ben, make sure you play 'Take My Hand, Precious Lord' in the meeting tonight. Play it real pretty," King said. Then, at 6:01 p.m., as he stood on the hotel balcony, a shot rang out. King was struck in the face with a single bullet, which tore the right side of his face and broke his jaw and spine. Although he was rushed to St. Joseph's Hospital, he died just an hour later, at 7:05 p.m.

The trial that followed King's death found a man named James Earl Ray guilty of the assassination. At the time of the shooting, Ray was seen running away from a hotel across the street from the Lorraine. A package was also found near the scene of the crime that included a gun with Ray's fingerprints on it. He was sentenced to 99 years in jail. Ray died in jail, when he was 70 years old.

However, new information since King's death has led people to question whether Ray was the real killer. Today, some believe King's death was part of a government plan. The answer is a mystery.

17.

Apollo 13

The story of Apollo 13 may be the world's second-most famous space flight, topped only by man's first walk on the moon. The Apollo Space Program was started by President John F. Kennedy in 1963. Apollo 13 was the seventh manned flight in the Apollo Space Program, and its purpose was to be the third moon landing in the history of the world. However, things went terribly wrong.

Before Apollo 13 even left Earth, there were problems. Just one week before Apollo 13 was supposed to launch, one of the astronauts had to be replaced because he came into contact with German measles, an illness that could have affected his ability to fly. The final three-man team who would fly Apollo 13 was Jim Lovell, Jr., John Swigert, Jr., and Fred Haise, Jr.

Apollo 13 launched from Kennedy Space Center in Florida at 2:13 p.m. on April 11, 1970. The first two days in space went smoothly, with only slight problems. However, after about 56 hours in space, an oxygen tank in the service module exploded, causing another oxygen tank to fail. This was just the first event in a chain of failures that almost cost the astronauts their lives.

Warning lights came on telling the astronauts that two of their three energy cells in the service module had failed. This was a major problem because all of the service module's electricity came from these cells. Without oxygen or electricity, the astronauts could not use or be in the command/service module—they would have to move to an extra space on Apollo 13 called the lunar module. In addition, the ground control team would have to figure out a way for the astronauts to save air, water, and energy, as well as a way for them to get home immediately.

Ground control at the NASA office in Houston, Texas, worked around the clock to figure out how to get the astronauts safely home. Before they could give any instructions to the astronauts, however, they had to test each step to see if they would work in space. They sent instructions to Lovell, Swigert, and Haise to drink very little water, and to turn off all the heating systems to save power. But the astronauts also noticed that the carbon dioxide build-up inside Apollo 13 was starting to reach dangerous levels. Although the spaceship had special machines to remove carbon dioxide from the air, the square machines that were used in the command module would not fit the circle openings in the lunar module.

Using only the materials that the astronauts would have in the spaceship, ground control figured out a way to fit the square machines onto the circle openings. They sent instructions to the astronauts, and they were able to fix the carbon dioxide problem using just plastic bags, tape, and cardboard.

Finally, ground control and the astronauts had to do some very difficult math to figure out how Apollo 13, which was on a course to land on the moon, could turn around and come back to Earth. As Apollo 13 went around the moon, the astronauts lined up a course using the position of the sun and were able to get on a course to return home. Finally, on April 17, 1970, Apollo 13 landed in the Pacific Ocean near Samoa. Lovell, Swigert, and Haise were not able to complete their mission to the moon, but they returned home safe.

18.

Three Mile Island

The accident that occurred at the Three Mile Island Nuclear Power Plant in Pennsylvania is famous for being the worst nuclear accident in the United States. But it is also famous for reportedly causing zero cases of cancer. In this sense, it was perhaps the cleanest nuclear disaster ever.

Everything was operating normally on March 28, 1979. Workers at the plant were going about their business as usual. But for reasons that are still unknown, a part of the plant that allowed water into the cooling tower stopped working at 4 a.m. With no water to cool the reactors, pressure and heat built up to dangerous levels. Radioactive materials were melting within the plant for several hours before workers realized there was a problem.

At 7 a.m., a plant worker declared a state of emergency at the plant. About thirty minutes later, a public state of emergency was declared to nearby cities. Workers were not sure how much radioactive matter was being released by the accident, and they worked quickly to reduce the heat in the plant. They got the cooling system working again, and the temperature in the reactor slowly came down. But the governor of Pennsylvania recommended that people living near the power plant leave the area. More than 140,000 people left the area within a few days. However, 98 percent of these people returned home within a few weeks.

Although plant workers successfully got the accident under control within the next week, the event created a strong feeling of fear and opposition against nuclear power among the

American people. Today, many people are against such power plants.

19.

The Murder of John Lennon

Perhaps no other death of a rock'n'roll star has shocked or saddened the world more than the murder of John Lennon. He was considered more than just a musician—he was an artist, poet, and activist—and his death has been considered the loss of one of the world's most creative minds at the time.

At the time of his death, John Lennon was living with his wife, Yoko Ono, at the now-famous The Dakota in New York City. On the day of December 8, 1980, the photographer Annie Liebovitz came to John and Yoko's apartment at The Dakota. She took photos of the couple for Rolling Stone magazine. One of the photos she took that day would become one of the most famous photos of the couple: it shows a naked John holding and kissing Yoko, all dressed in black, as they lay on the ground.

Liebovitz left the apartment at around 3:30 p.m. John then gave what would be his very last interview, which was later played on the radio. After the interview, at about 5:00 p.m., John and Yoko left their apartment and headed to the Record Plant Studio to record a song together. As the couple walked outside to their car, a few people waiting outside the apartment's gates asked for John's autograph. This happened quite often, and John greeted the people as he usually did.

One of the people was a 25-year-old man from Honolulu, Hawaii, named Mark David Chapman. Without saying anything, he handed John a copy of *Double Fantasy*, John's last record. John signed the record and gave it back, asking "Is this all you want?" Chapman smiled and nodded yes. After that, John and Yoko got into their car and drove off.

The couple returned to The Dakota at about 10:50 p.m. They wanted to say goodnight to their five-year-old son, Sean, before they headed out again for dinner.

John and Yoko got out of their car at The Dakota's 72nd Street entrance. Yoko walked ahead of John and entered the apartment. John followed a little bit behind, and he noticed a man standing in the shadows. He walked on, and the man stepped forward. It was Chapman. He pointed a gun at John's back and fired five times.

John managed to walk up five steps to the reception area and told the man at the desk, "I'm shot, I'm shot." He was bleeding from his mouth. He fell to the floor. The man immediately called the police and looked to John's wounds. Outside, the guard at the door shook the gun from Chapman's hand and kicked the gun away. Chapman knew the police would arrive shortly, so he took off his jacket and his hat to show that he was not carrying any other guns. Then he sat down quietly on the street to wait for the police. In his hands he held a copy of the book, *The Catcher in the Rye.*

Two police teams arrived, and one team took Chapman away as the other team rushed John to the hospital. Although the doctors at Roosevelt Hospital tried all they could to help John, he was dead on arrival. John Lennon was declared dead at 11:15 p.m. When the doctors gave Yoko the news, she fell to the ground and began to cry. In her state of shock, she had to be led away from the hospital by David Geffen, the president of Geffen Records.

The next day, Yoko made a public statement: "There is no funeral for John. John loved and prayed for the human race. Please do the same for him. Love, Yoko and Sean."

Although there was no funeral, the world responded in a huge showing of grief. On December 14, 1980, millions of people around the world joined to observe 10 minutes of silence for John Lennon. Every radio station in New York City was silent for 10 minutes. Chapman was sentenced to life in prison, where he still lives today.

20.

Chernobyl

The Chernobyl Nuclear Power Plant disaster occurred in 1986. It is considered the worst nuclear-power accident in history. Chernobyl and the Fukushima Daiichi disaster of 2011 were the only two Level 7 (highest level) nuclear accidents in the world.

Chernobyl, a nuclear power plant, was located in Ukraine, near Belarus. The plant was going through a normal test of its systems on April 26, 1986, when things went terribly wrong. At 1:23 a.m., a sudden power surge at the plant caused nuclear reactor number four to explode. Workers immediately tried to shut down the plant, but the systems to close and contain the radioactive matter did not work. While fires broke out all over reactor number four, great amounts of radioactive matter were released into the air.

Local firefighters rushed to the scene within five minutes, and more arrived until the fires were all put out. They had to work quickly to make sure the fire did not spread to the other reactors. Although the fires were all out by about 6:30 a.m., the radioactive fire inside reactor number four continued to burn for about two weeks. There was nothing anyone could do to stop this.

Some of the firefighters who rushed to the power plant died either from the fire or from radiation sickness. Some said they did not know the fire was radioactive, while others said they knew but they rushed to the scene anyway.

It took more than 500,000 workers to clean up the Chernobyl accident and to contain its dangerous effects. However, the disaster still introduced so much radiation into the surrounding area that the radiation levels in Sweden, over 1,600 kilometers away, were dangerously high. The Soviet government had to move the entire population of 350,400 people who lived in the city of Pripyat, where the plant was located, to a different city. Those people were never allowed to return home, and the entire city of Pripyat is still blocked off today.

The effects of the Chernobyl accident still continues. The Russian government says that only 31 people died as a direct result of the accident, but many people say the government did not reporting correct numbers. Ukraine alone reported 5,722 people who died or became sick after the accident. The accident continues to cause serious illnesses among populations live nearby today.

21.

The Death of Princess Diana

Princess Diana was a widely popular member of British royalty. Born into a noble family, Diana Spencer was Lady Diana Spencer until she married Charles, Prince of Wales, in 1981. Then she became Diana, Princess of Wales. Although Diana was well-loved by society, her marriage to Prince Charles was difficult and she was a deeply unhappy person. Her marriage ended in divorce in 1996. She died suddenly in a car accident just a year later, causing shock and grief across the world. Some say the accident was a planned event meant to assassinate her.

Diana Spencer grew up with unhappy parents. Her mother and father divorced when she was eight years old. After her parents' separation, Diana lived with her father for a time but was sent off to boarding school. She was not a very good student, but she was a good musician. She was also very good with children, and after finishing school, she became a pre-school teacher.

Diana met Prince Charles in 1977. He was dating Diana's older sister, Sarah, at the time. However, in the summer of 1980, the two met again during a weekend polo game, and they began to date. Charles asked Diana to marry him on February 6, 1981. She accepted.

Diana and Charles were married on July 29, 1981, when Diana was 20 years old. Charles was in his early thirties. Diana had their first son, William, less than a year later. A second son, Henry, followed in two years. Diana was a very devoted mother and became more popular around the world for always making time for her children, even while performing her many duties as the Princess of Wales. However, Diana was not happy with her marriage, and neither was Charles. They both had affairs, which were made public in May 1992. In December 1992, the royal couple decided to spend some time apart. They spent the next five years separated. The media continued to report on the separation of the royal couple, never letting them keep their private lives to themselves. The couple officially divorced in 1996.

After her divorce, Diana spent much of her time doing charity work around the world. She became ever more popular. She also dated other men. But it all came suddenly to an end on August 31, 1997.

Diana had just returned from a vacation with her boyfriend, Dodi Fayed. They were on their way to London, but first they were going to stay one night in Paris at Dodi's father's apartment. The couple and their body guard was being driven to the apartment. It was midnight, and the couple's black Mercedes was being followed by paparazzi. Then, just a few minutes into the drive, the driver lost control of the car. The car crashed into a pole, then into a wall and came to a stop. The crash killed the driver instantly. Dodi, however, was hurt but still alive, as was Diana.

At the time of the crash, the paparazzi who were nearby continued to take pictures rather than help. When the emergency team arrived, they tried to treat Diana and Dodi on the spot. By 1:30 a.m., Dodi had died. The crash caused Diana to have a heart attack. She was rushed to the hospital, but she died at 4 a.m.

When news of Diana's death was made public, the entire world reacted with grief. About 3 million people gathered near Westminster Abbey for her funeral on September 6. Millions more around the world watched the funeral on television. She was buried at her childhood home of Althorp Park.

22.

9/11

Tuesday, September 11, 2001, is a day that changed American history. On the morning of September 11, the largest terrorist attack against the United States was carried out. It is also the only terrorist attack against the United States that occurred on American soil. The event shocked the world and caused a war in Iraq, which lasted almost ten years. It finally led to the assassination of Osama bin Laden, the leader of the Islamist terrorist group, al-Qaeda. The attack forever changed the way the American people think about foreign policy, the

international role of the U.S., and terrorism.

The terrorist attack of September 11 took the form of four suicide attacks. Nineteen al-Qaeda terrorists took control of four American airplanes with the purpose of crashing them into buildings in New York City and Washington, D.C. These events took place within the space of two hours on a Tuesday morning. What happened is known today as 9/11.

It seemed to be a normal Tuesday morning, similar to any other morning in the late summer. But at 8:45 a.m., an airplane carrying 92 passengers crashed into the north World Trade Center tower in New York. About 15 minutes later, a second plane carrying 65 people crashed into the south World Trade Center tower. As the city of New York went into total shock, word spread throughout the country that the United States was under attack.

Roughly half an hour after the second attack, at 9:40 a.m., a third plane carrying 64 people crashed into the Pentagon in Washington, D.C., which is the home of the U.S. Department of Defense. Twenty minutes later, at 10:03 a.m., a fourth plane carrying 40 people crashed into a field in Pennsylvania about 80 miles southeast of Pittsburgh.

As the World Trade Center towers caught on fire and sent great clouds of smoke into the air, people across the world watched the terrible images on television in complete shock. Never before had such a thing happened in the United States. The U.S., considered a strong nation, had never been attacked like this. Now, somebody with a dark plan was proving that the U.S. could be weak too.

Both World Trade Center towers fell down within two hours. The Pentagon was seriously damaged. Nearly 3,000 people died in these four terrorist attacks. Among the people who died, many died as heroes. Almost 400 New York firefighters and police officers died while trying to save people.

Flight 93, which people now believe was supposed to crash into the U.S. Capitol in Washington, D.C., crashed instead into a field in Pennsylvania because of the brave acts of the passengers. Realizing that the plane had been hijacked, some of the passengers fought back. Although everybody died in the crash, the passengers' actions saved damage to the nation's Capitol.

George W. Bush, who was president of the U.S. at the time, reacted to the attacks by ordering a "War on Terror." The U.S. government attacked Afghanistan, aiming to break up the Taliban, which is known to support al Qaeda. This then led to the U.S. war against Iraq. Many countries around the world looked down on this move as useless and badly planned.

A year after the September 11 attacks, in November 2002, Osama bin Laden, a leader of al-Qaeda, wrote his "Letter to America." In the letter, bin Laden said he and other al-Qaeda members had planned 9/11 as a way to punish

America for their terrible treatment of Muslims and the Arab world. He said Americans had been stealing from Arab countries and taking advantage of its people for years. Osama bin Laden then became the top target for the U.S. "War on Terror." A full-scale hunt for bin Laden began.

Ten years later, President Barack Obama became the man to command the military operation to kill Osama bin Laden. On May 2, 2011, bin Laden was killed by American special forces in Pakistan.

The painful memories of September 11 still affect the American people. Many hope for a future in which such death, terror, and hate against fellow humans does not exist.

23.

Tesla Unveils
the Model Y

On March 14, 2019, Tesla, the automotive industry's leader in electric vehicles, unveiled its new Model Y, an even better version of the Model 3 introduced in 2016, with a range of more than 500 kilometers per charge.

In order to prevent global warming, the automobile industry has been working hard to switch over to electric vehicles. In this context, Tesla, which was founded as a venture company in 2003 and has been experimenting with the idea of fully automated driving using electric vehicles and AI, has become a major threat to the rest of the global automobile industry since the release of the Model 3. This is because there is a growing movement in the U.S. and Europe to eliminate gasoline-powered cars by 2035, and Tesla is considered to be the most technologically advanced company in terms of this goal.

In fact, it has been reported in various media outlets in the 2020s that Tesla is profitable and that its sales are starting to grow rapidly.

If one were to say that "innovation in self-driving and the development of electric vehicles is inevitable for the auto industry in the future," everyone would agree. However, many people do not realize that there has been an even more important development in the industry.

What Tesla is trying to do may cause a major paradigm shift in the industry, just like Steve Jobs' attempt to revolutionize the way we think about phones and computers through the iPhone and personal computer.

To understand the significance of Tesla's technology, you need to know the term "neural network." These are simulations of the networks of neurons in the human brain, and are designed to recognize patterns. They are able to improve through experience, and make decisions based on the input they receive. This important technology will determine the future of AI. While it is working both on self-driving and improving the vehicles themselves, Tesla has been the most focused on innovation in the former.

Many thought that in order to be able to drive automatically, a supercomputer should be able to memorize real roads, buildings, and signs in three dimensions, and then incorporate this vast amount of data into a car's functions. The auto industry was also strategizing the use of neural network technology to help the car see things and operate the steering wheel and brakes. That's how difficult it was for a computer to acquire the same vision as a human. However, Tesla, with its Dojo supercomputer, has taken on the challenge of developing a neural network-based self-driving car.

This tells us that Tesla is not just an auto-maker that specializes in self-driving cars. The technology behind Tesla, which is concentrated in places like Silicon Valley, is about to become a resource for fostering a new industry that goes beyond just manufacturing vehicles.

Many investors in the U.S. are now bitterly criticizing traditional Wall Street investors for only valuing Tesla as a car company. What we need to understand is that Tesla is not a car company, but a pioneer company trying to break new ground in AI. The problem is that the challenges of industry in general are very similar to this classic Wall Street thinking.

It's important to realize that the neural networks used in self-driving cars will bring about changes that affect much more than just the auto industry.

For a long time, the housing market has been used as an indicator to predict the future of the economy. This is because when more houses are built, sold, and bought, the demand for various products, such as home appliances, increases, and even the finance and insurance industries can benefit from this.

Similarly, automobiles and aircraft are at the top of a wide range of industries, and just like with housing, it has been said that if these industries grow, the economy of the country itself will grow steadily. Needless to say, Japan and Germany have also followed this widely accepted idea to achieve their current economic status.

However, the reputation of key industries, such as housing and automobiles, which support such economies, is gradually changing. Tesla is a perfect symbol of this.

To understand this, we need to look at the fact that Tesla was only able to grow because of AI solutions such as Dojo.

Or to put it another way, the diverse technologies and artificial intelligences in Silicon Valley and elsewhere are becoming more than subcontractors in the manufacture of a single product like the automobile. These technology and artificial intelligence companies are no longer component manufacturers. They are going to reign over housing and automobiles as companies that provide solutions, as exemplified by neural network technology. It is only with these AI-supported technologies and solutions that a wide variety of products can be created, and automobiles are about to become just one of many such product groups.

Unless the traditional automobile industry understands this reality and expands its innovation network to the world, it may not be able to develop new products. Therefore, a major shift in thinking is necessary in order for new automobiles, such as Teslas, to be born. If the technology of automated driving and the know-how of electric vehicle production do not complement and integrate with each other, it will be impossible for either to succeed.

Tesla is now aiming to build production bases not only in the U.S. but also in Europe and China, and is also trying to develop an infrastructure network for vehicle production in Eurasia. Needless to say, it is also trying to lead the world in developing a network of charging facilities for electric vehicles. This was also true when the telegraph was invented. A network of poles and wires was required so that people could use the new machines. AI technology solutions are altering global infrastructure itself.

Against this backdrop, it is important to note that even more than territorial and military hegemony, AI technology hegemony has become the most important issue in international politics. It may not be long before automakers become subcontractors for AIs.

In the 19th century, it was railroads, in the 20th century it was automobiles, and in the 21st century, it will be the invisible AIs that will lead other industries.

24.

The U.S. Capitol Riot

No election in recent years has captured the world's attention more than the 2020 presidential race in the United States.

President Trump abandoned the U.S. policy of cooperation with the rest of the world, as is clear from his global warming policy, and changed various conventional policies under the slogan "America First." Former vice president Joe Biden of the Democratic Party felt threatened by Trump's rightward-leaning tendencies, and the two went head-to-head against each other. It was a fierce battle that split the nation in two.

In the middle of an election campaign, the May 2020 protests in Minnesota over the killing of a black citizen, George Floyd, by a white police officer, and the debate over the government's measures to deal with the death toll of the coronavirus, which has now surpassed 600,000, also brought unprecedented tension to the campaign.

Although Biden won the election by a margin of 8 million votes, dissatisfied voters staged mass protests claiming that the election was rigged.

On January 6, 2021, an unprecedented incident occurred: a mob of Trump supporters broke into the U.S. Capitol in Washington, D.C., and attempted to prevent Congress from formally approving the president-elect by force. The rioters even broke into one of the chambers, resulting in casualties.

Generally speaking, riots are thought of as something that the needy or people suffering from discrimination do when they cannot stand oppression or inequality. However, these riots were started by radical supporters of President Trump, who came from all over the U.S. using their own funds. They were not the needy or the unfairly treated.

They wanted to bring the United States back to their idea of "America" through the policies promoted by Trump. The intruders were a radicalized group of ardent supporters of the president, who tolerated a heavily armed society, were anti-immigration, and rejected traditional policies, such as the elimination of racial discrimination.

This is what you need to know to put this incident into perspective. It's about the right of Americans to own guns, which has been a social issue for many years now. This is because the idea behind this right and the current riots are connected by an invisible thread.

The origin of the right to bear arms can be traced back to the time when the United States gained independence from Great Britain. In the Declaration of Independence, an inspiration for the current U.S. Constitution, there is a section that says that if any government fails to recognize the right of the people to equality and the pursuit of happiness, or shall act against those interests, the people have the right to remove that government and institute a new one. This right to overthrow the government is called the "right of revolution," and its origins can be traced back to the 17th century in Western Europe. The right of citizens to challenge the government was considered to be a fundamental one.

This right to revolution and the right to defend one's life and property that underlies it are still embedded in the hearts and minds of the people, and they underpin the right to bear arms in the United States. Regardless of who started the riots, the reason there are so many protests against the suppression of the right to bear arms in the U.S. is that the idea that the individual can challenge the government is strongly rooted in the American consciousness.

However, this action must be firmly distinguished from other protests, as it threatens the very foundation of the rule of law, and most politicians, as well as the media, criticized those who broke into the Capitol.

Immediately after the incident, the U.S. Congress was extremely angry at President Trump for inciting the riots. It even went so far as to call for his removal from office, even though he only had a short time left in his term.

This was a response to the 25th Amendment to the U.S. Constitution, which states that if the government and Congress deem the president unfit to discharge the duties of his office, he or she shall be removed from office, and the vice president shall be appointed president. However, this procedure required the cooperation of the cabinet members, including Vice President Pence and the approval of Congress, it was ultimately not used due to opposition from the Republican Party, which President Trump belongs to.

Whether or not President Trump was involved in the riots is still the subject of a major investigation.

In the United States, there have been various divisions in society, such as the gap between rich and poor, racial tensions, and conflicts between long-time residents and new immigrants. These divisions created conflict between the Republican Party, which had yielded to Trump and the conservative base that elected him, and the Democratic Party, which had been more tolerant of immigrants and had taken a strong stance against racism, finally leading to this major incident.

Just prior to this event, Georgia was holding a runoff election for the U.S. Senate. As a result, Democratic candidates won the two seats that were contested in the traditionally conservative state of Georgia. As a result of this series of elections, at the start of the Biden Administration, the Democrats had the upper hand in both the Senate and the House of Representatives. From the Democrats' point of view, this was an unprecedented accomplishment.

Angered by these new developments in the political world, radical Trump supporters went on a rampage, taking over Congress.

In fact, many Americans say that the riots were predictable, as the society is divided. The response of the FBI and the police was also criticized, with many wondering why the security at the Capitol was not tighter. Of course, there must have been many people who thought that those who participated in the riots were from some other universe that we can never understand. However, according to the FBI and other authorities, most of the people who participated in the riots were ordinary citizens. Moreover, even individuals who had served in the U.S. military and had combat experience participated, so the situation was very serious. In other words, the division among American citizens had become extremely deep-rooted.

What they really want, and what President Trump really wants, is a backlash against the diversity and variety of American society, said a liberal who supports the Democratic Party. In other words, there is a hidden idea in their minds that people of color, non-Christians, and many immigrants are undermining American society, and their true feelings have exploded into mob violence.

What the FBI is extremely concerned about now is not terrorist attacks from outside the country by Islamic fundamentalists like in the case of 9/11, but acts of terrorism secretly planned by seemingly ordinary American citizens against the president, his government, and even people with whom they disagree. And people are wary that the brunt of it will be directed at the federal government facilities and other public places as a result of the distortion of the right of revolution mentioned above.

Later, those who instigated and carried out the break-in at the Capitol were arrested and charged with crimes, receiving harsh sentences, including 40 months in prison. However, the social unrest created by the division of the United States is unlikely to abate in the future.

Word List

A

□ **abandon** 图①自暴自棄 ②気まま, 奔放 動①捨てる, 放棄する ②(計画などを)中止する, 断念する

□ **abate** 動 (痛みなどが)和らぐ, (痛みなどを)和らげる

□ **abbey** 图 修道院

□ **abhor** 動 (ひどく)嫌う

□ **ability** 图①できること, (〜する)能力 ②才能

□ **aboard** 副 船[列車・飛行機・バス]に乗って 前 〜に乗って

□ **about** 熟 about to《be –》まさに〜しようとしている bring about 引き起こす

□ **Abraham Lincoln** エイブラハム・リンカーン《第16代アメリカ合衆国大統領, 任期1861–1865》

□ **Academy Award for Best Picture** アカデミー作品賞

□ **accept** 動①受け入れる ②同意する, 認める

□ **accident** 图①(不慮の)事故, 災難 ②偶然 by accident 偶然に

□ **accommodate** 動①収容する ②適合させる, 合わせる

□ **accompany** 動①ついていく, つきそう ②(〜に)ともなって起こる ③伴奏をする

□ **accomplishment** 图①完成, 達成 ②業績

□ **according** 副《– to〜》〜によれば[よると]

□ **accumulate** 動①蓄積する, 積もる ②積み上げる, 積み重ねる

□ **achieve** 動 成し遂げる, 達成する, 成功を収める

□ **acquire** 動①(努力して)獲得する, 確保する ②(学力, 技術などを)習得する

□ **act** 图 行為, 行い 動 行動する

□ **activist** 图 活動家, 実践主義者

□ **activity** 图 活動, 活気

□ **actor** 图 俳優, 役者

□ **actually** 副 実際に, 本当に, 実は

□ **A.D.** 略 紀元後, 西暦〜年 (= anno Domini)

□ **ad** 略 advertisement (広告, 宣伝)の略

□ **addition** 图 付加, 追加 in addition 加えて, さらに

□ **address** 图 住所

□ **administration** 图 管理, 統治, 政権

□ **advanced** 動advance（進む）の過去，過去分詞 形上級の，先に進んだ，高等の

□ **advantage** 名有利な点［立場］，強み，優越 **take advantage of** ～を利用する，～につけ込む

□ **affair** 名不倫，浮気

□ **affect** 動影響する

□ **afford** 動《can –》～することができる，～する（経済的・時間的な）余裕がある

□ **Afghanistan** 名アフガニスタン《国》

□ **Africa** 名アフリカ《大陸》

□ **African-American** 名アフリカ系アメリカ人 形アフリカ系アメリカ人の

□ **after that** その後

□ **Age of Discovery** 《the –》大発見［航海］時代

□ **agent** 名①代理人 ②代表者

□ **ahead of** ～より先［前］に，～に先んじて

□ **AI** 略人工知能（＝artificial intelligence）

□ **aim** 動ねらう，目指す

□ **air** 熟disappear into thin air 虚空に消える

□ **Air Force One** エアフォースワン《アメリカ合衆国大統領専用機》

□ **aircraft** 名飛行機，航空機

□ **airfield** 名飛行場

□ **airplane** 名飛行機

□ **Alabama** 名アラバマ州

□ **Albert** 名アルバート《ジョージ6世，イギリス国王，在位1936–1952》

□ **Alexei** 名アレクセイ（・ニコラエヴィチ）《ニコライ2世第一皇子，1904–1918》

□ **all** 熟all over ～中で，～の至る所で **all over the world** 世界中に **first of all** まず第一に

□ **allow** 動①許す，《 – … to ～》…が～するのを可能にする，…に～させておく ②与える

□ **alone** 熟leave ～ alone ～をそっとしておく

□ **along** 熟along with ～と一緒に

□ **al-Qaeda** 名アルカイダ《世界規模で活動する反米・反イスラエルのテロ組織》

□ **alter** 動（部分的に）変える，変わる

□ **Althorp Park** オルソープ・パーク《地名，ノーサンプトン州，スペンサー家領地内》

□ **although** 接～だけれども，～にもかかわらず，たとえ～でも

□ **Amelia Earhart** アメリア・イアハート《アメリカの飛行士，1897–1937》

□ **amendment** 名①改正，修正 ②（憲法の）改正案

□ **America** 名アメリカ《国名・大陸》

□ **American** 形アメリカ（人）の 名アメリカ人

□ **American Revolution** アメリカ独立革命《1775年コンコードの戦いから1783年パリ条約までを指す》

□ **amount** 名量

□ **amusing** 動amuse（楽しませる）の現在分詞 形楽しくさせる，楽しい

□ **Anastasia** 名アナスタシア（・ニコラエヴナ）《ニコライ2世第三皇女，1901–1918》

□ **ancient** 形昔の，古代の

□ **anger** 名怒り 動怒る，～を怒らせる

□ **angry at** 《be –》～に腹を立てている

□ **Anita Snook** アニタ・（"ネタ"・）スヌーク《アイオワ州最初の女性飛行士，1896–1991》

□ **Anne Boleyn** アン・ブーリン《イングランド王ヘンリー8世の2番目の王妃（1533年結婚，1536年離婚）》

1507–1536》

- **Anne of Cleves** アン・オブ・クレーヴズ《イングランド王ヘンリー8世の4番目の王妃（1540年結婚，同年離婚）1515–1557》

- **Annie Liebovitz** アニー・リーボヴィッツ《アメリカ合衆国の写真家，1949–》

- **announce** 動（人に）知らせる，公表する

- **anti-immigration** 名反移民，移民排斥 形反移民の，移民反対［排斥］の

- **any** if any もしあれば，あったとしても

- **anybody** 代①《疑問文・条件節で》誰か ②《否定文で》誰も（～ない）③《肯定文で》誰でも **anybody who ～** する人はだれでも

- **anymore** 副《通例否定文，疑問文で》今はもう，これ以上，これから

- **anyone** 代①《疑問文・条件節で》誰か ②《否定文で》誰も（～ない）③《肯定文で》誰でも

- **anyway** 副①いずれにせよ，ともかく ②どんな方法でも

- **apart** 副①ばらばらに，離れて ②別にして，それだけで

- **apartment** 名アパート

- **Apollo 13** アポロ13号

- **Apollo Space Program** アポロ計画《アメリカ航空宇宙局（NASA）による人類初の月への有人宇宙飛行計画，1961–1972》

- **appear** 動現れる，見えてくる

- **appearance** 名外見，印象

- **appoint** 動①任命する，指名する ②（日時・場所などを）指定する

- **approach** 動接近する

- **approval** 名①賛成 ②承認，認可

- **approve** 動賛成する，承認する

- **apron** 名エプロン

- **Arab** 名アラビア人，アラブ民族，アラブ 形アラブ（人）の

- **ardent** 形熱心な，熱烈な

- **Arlington National Cemetery** アーリントン国立墓地

- **armed** 形武装した，武器を持った

- **army** 名軍隊，《the –》陸軍

- **arrange** 動準備する，手はずを整える

- **arrest** 動逮捕する 名逮捕

- **arrival** 名①到着 ②到達

- **arrive in** ～に着く

- **Arthur C. Clarke** アーサー・C・クラーク《イギリス出身のSF作家・科学評論家，1917–2008》

- **artificial** 形①人工的な ②不自然な，わざとらしい

- **artificial intelligence** 人工知能（＝AI）

- **artist** 名芸術家

- **as** 熟 **as a matter of fact** 実際は，実のところ **as a result** その結果（として）**as a result of** ～の結果（として）**as if** あたかも～のように，まるで～みたいに **as long as** ～する以上は，～である限りは **as soon as** ～するとすぐ，～するや否や **as to** ～に関しては，～については **as usual** いつものように，相変わらず **as well** その上，同様に **as well as** ～と同様に **just as** （ちょうど）であろうとおり **known as**《be –》～として知られている **see ～ as …** ～を…と考える **so ～ as to …** …するほど～で **such as** たとえば～，～のような **the same ～ as［that］…** …と同じ（ような）**thought of as**《be –》～（である）と考えられる

- **Asia** 名アジア

- **assassinate** 動暗殺する

- **assassination** 名暗殺

- **assume** 動①仮定する，当然のことと思う ②引き受ける

□ **astronaut** 图宇宙飛行士

□ **Atlantic** 形大西洋の 图《the –》大西洋

□ **attack** 動襲う, 攻める 图①攻撃, 非難 ②発作, 発病 **heart attack** 心臓麻痺 **be under attack** 攻撃を受ける

□ **attacker** 图攻撃者, 敵

□ **attempt** 動試みる, 企てる 图試み, 企て, 努力

□ **attend** 動出席する

□ **attention** 图①注意, 集中 ②配慮, 手当て, 世話

□ **Austria** 图オーストリア《国名》

□ **authority** 图①権威, 権力, 権限 ②《the -ties》(関係) 当局

□ **auto industry** 自動車工業 [産業]

□ **autograph** 图 (有名人の) サイン

□ **automaker** 图自動車メーカー

□ **automated** 形〔機械・コンピューターなどによって作業・仕事が〕オートメーション化された

□ **automatically** 副無意識に, 自動的に, 惰性的に

□ **automobile** 图自動車

□ **automotive** 形①自動車の ②自動推進の

□ **award** 图賞, 賞品

□ **aware** 形①気がついて, 知って ②(の) 認識のある

□ **awoken** 動 awake (目覚めさせる) の過去分詞

B

□ **back** 熟 **bring back** 戻す, 呼び戻す

□ **backdrop** 图背景

□ **backlash** 图〔政治的・社会的な〕出来事や傾向に対する強い〕反発, 反感

□ **badly** 副①悪く, まずく, へたに ②とても, ひどく

□ **Baghdad** 图バグダッド《イラクの首都》

□ **balcony** 图①バルコニー ②桟敷, 階上席

□ **band** 图楽団

□ **Barack Obama** バラク・オバマ《第44代アメリカ合衆国大統領, 任期 2009~2017》

□ **barbaric** 形〔人・態度・行為などが〕野蛮な, 粗野な, 残酷な ②〔場所などが〕未開の

□ **barely** 副①かろうじて, やっと ②ほぼ, もう少しで

□ **base** 图基礎, 土台, 本部 動《– on ~》~に基礎を置く, 基づく

□ **bathroom** 图①浴室 ②手洗い, トイレ

□ **battle** 图戦闘, 戦い 動戦う

□ **Battle of Tours**《the –》トゥール・ポワティエ間の戦い《732年にフランス西部のトゥールとポワティエの間で起こった, フランク王国とウマイヤ朝による戦い》

□ **bear** 動①運ぶ ②支える ③耐える ④有する

□ **beat** 動打つ

□ **beauty** 图美, 美しい人 [物]

□ **because of** ~のために, ~の理由で

□ **before** 熟 **like never before** かつてないほど

□ **begin** 熟 **begin with** ~で始まる **to begin with** はじめに, まず第一に

□ **beginning** 動 begin (始まる) の現在分詞 图初め, 始まり

□ **behead** 動 (処刑で) 首をはねる

□ **beheading** 图断頭

□ **behind** 前①~の後ろに, ~の背後に ②~に劣って, ~に遅れて 副①後ろに, 背後に ②遅れて, 劣って

□ **being** 動 be（〜である）の現在分詞 名存在, 生命, 人間

□ **Belarus** 名ベラルーシ共和国

□ **Belfast** 名ベルファスト《北アイルランドの首都》

□ **belief** 名信じること, 信念, 信用

□ **belong** 動《 – to 〜》〜に属する, 〜のものである

□ **Ben Branch** ベン・ブランチ《ジャズ・ミュージシャン, 1924-1987》

□ **benefit** 名①利益, 恩恵 ②（失業保険・年金などの）手当, 給付（金）動利益を得る,（〜の）ためになる

□ **bent** 動 bend（曲がる）の過去, 過去分詞

□ **best-loved** 形最も愛される

□ **Betty Gow** ベティ・ガウ《子守り, 本名Bessie Mowat Gow, 1904-?》

□ **between A and B** AとBの間に

□ **beyond** 前〜を越えて, 〜の向こうに 副向こうに

□ **Biden** 名《Joe – 》ジョー・バイデン《アメリカ合衆国第46代大統領（2021-）, 1942-》

□ **bill** 名紙幣

□ **birth** 名出産, 誕生 give birth to 〜を生む

□ **bit** 名《a – 》少し, ちょっと

□ **bitterly** 副激しく, 苦々しく

□ **Black Death** 《the – 》黒死病《1340年代後半にユーラシアと北アフリカでパンデミックを起こした腺ペストの俗称》

□ **blackening** 名黒くすること[もの]

□ **bleed** 動出血する, 血を流す[流せる]

□ **bleeding** 名出血 internal bleeding 内出血

□ **blink** 名[目の]まばたき in the blink of an eye 瞬く間に, あっという間に

□ **blood** 名①血, 血液 ②血統, 家柄 ③気質

□ **bloody** 形血だらけの, 血なまぐさい, むごい

□ **Bloody Mary** ブラッディ・メアリー（血まみれのメアリー）《イングランド女王メアリー1世の異名, 在位1553-1558》

□ **boarding school** 寄宿制[全寮制]の学校

□ **Boccaccio** 名ボッカチオ《中世イタリアの詩人・散文作家, 1313-1375》

□ **Bohemia** 名ボヘミア《歴史的地名, ポーランド南部からチェコ北部にかけた地方》

□ **Bonnie Parker** ボニー・パーカー《1910-1934》

□ **booth** 名ブース, 売店, 切符売り場

□ **border** 名境界, へり, 国境 動①接する, 境をなす ②縁どりをつける

□ **bored** 形うんざりした, 退屈した

□ **both A and B** AもBも

□ **bottom** 名底, 下部

□ **bound** 形《 – for 〜》〜行きの

□ **boyfriend** 名男友だち

□ **brain** 名①脳 ②知力

□ **brake** 名ブレーキ, 歯止め 動ブレーキ[歯止め]をかける

□ **brave** 形勇敢な

□ **break-in** 名力ずくで入り込む, 押し入る, 乱入する

□ **break into** 〜に押し入る, 急に〜する

□ **break out** 発生する, 急に起こる,（戦争が）勃発する

□ **break up** ばらばらになる, 解散させる

□ **bring about** 引き起こす

□ **bring back** 戻す, 呼び戻す

□ **British** 形英国（人）の

□ **British Empire** 大英帝国

- □ **Bronx** 名 ブロンクス《ニューヨーク市の区》
- □ **Bruno Richard Hauptmann** ブルーノ・リチャード・ハウプトマン《ドイツ系移民の大工, 1899–1936》
- □ **brunt** 名 ①〔打撃などの〕衝撃 ②〔攻撃の〕矛先
- □ **Brussels** 名 ブリュッセル《ベルギーの首都》
- □ **building** 名 建物, 建造物, ビルディング
- □ **build-up** 積み上がった
- □ **bullet** 名 銃弾, 弾丸状のもの
- □ **bump** 名 こぶ, 隆起
- □ **burn** 動 焼く, 燃やす
- □ **bury** 動 (遺体を)葬る, 埋葬する
- □ **business** 熟 go about business as usual 普段どおりに仕事をする
- □ **businessmen** 名 businessman (ビジネスマン)の複数
- □ **but** 熟 not only ~ but (also) … ~だけでなく…もまた not ~ but … ~ではなくて…

C

- □ **cabinet** 名 ①飾り棚 ②《-s》内閣, 閣僚
- □ **California** 名 カリフォルニア《米国の州》
- □ **call for** ~を求める, 訴える
- □ **calling card** 名刺
- □ **campaign** 名 ①キャンペーン(活動, 運動) ②政治運動, 選挙運動 ③軍事行動 動 ①従軍する ②運動に参加する
- □ **cancel** 動 取り消す, 中止する
- □ **cancer** 名 癌
- □ **candidate** 名 ①立候補者 ②学位取得希望者 ③志願者
- □ **Capitol** 名 米国の国会議事堂

- □ **captain** 名 大尉
- □ **capture** 動 捕える 名 捕えること, 捕獲(物)
- □ **carbon** 名 炭素
- □ **carbon dioxide** 二酸化炭素
- □ **card paper** ボール紙
- □ **cardboard** 名 ボール紙, 厚紙
- □ **care** 熟 take good care of ~を大事に扱う, 大切にする
- □ **career** 名 ①(生涯の・専門的な)職業 ②経歴, キャリア
- □ **Carpathia** 名 カルパチア《外洋客船。タイタニック号遭難事件で生存者の救助に当たった》
- □ **carry on** 続ける
- □ **carry out** 外へ運び出す, [計画を]実行する
- □ **cart** 名 荷車
- □ **case** 熟 case of ~の例 in the case of ~の場合は
- □ **casualty** 名 死傷者, 犠牲者
- □ **catch on fire** 燃えだす
- □ **Catcher in the Rye** 『ライ麦畑でつかまえて』《J・D・サリンジャー著の小説, 1951》
- □ **cathedral** 名 大聖堂
- □ **Catherine Howard** キャサリン・ハワード《イングランド王ヘンリー8世の5番目の王妃(1540年結婚, 1542年離婚), 1521?–1542》
- □ **Catherine of Aragon** キャサリン・オブ・アラゴン《イングランド王ヘンリー8世の最初の王妃(1509年結婚, 1533年離婚), 1487–1536》
- □ **Catherine Parr** キャサリン・パー《イングランド王ヘンリー8世の6人目かつ最後の王妃(1543年結婚, 1547年死別), 1512–1548》
- □ **Catholic** 形 カトリックの 名 カトリック教徒
- □ **Catholic Church** カトリック教会

125

□ **Catholicism** 名 カトリック教義 [信仰]

□ **cattle** 名 畜牛, 家畜

□ **celebration** 名 ①祝賀 ②祝典, 儀式

□ **cell** 名 電池

□ **cemetery** 名 共同墓地

□ **certainly** 副 確かに, 必ず

□ **chain of** 一連の〜

□ **chairman** 名 委員長, 会長, 議長

□ **challenge** 名 ①挑戦 ②難問 動 挑む, 試す

□ **chamber** 名 部屋, 室

□ **charge** 動 (〜を…に) 負わせる **be charged with** 〜の罪で告発される

□ **charity** 名 慈善 (行為)

□ **Charlemagne** 名 シャルルマーニュ《またはカール大帝, フランク王国の国王・初代神聖ローマ皇帝 (742?–814)》

□ **Charles Augustus Lindbergh, Jr.** チャールズ・オーガスタス・リンドバーグ・ジュニア《チャールズ・リンドバーグの長男, 1930–1932》

□ **Charles Lindbergh** チャールズ・(オーガスタス・) リンドバーグ《アメリカの飛行家, 1902–1974》

□ **Charles Martel** カール・マルテル《メロヴィング朝フランク王国の宮宰, 688?–741》

□ **Charles, Prince of Wales** チャールズ (プリンス・オブ・ウェールズ)《エリザベス2世第一王子, 現国王チャールズ3世 (2022–), 1948–》

□ **charm** 動 魅了する

□ **check** 動 照合する, 検査する **check on** 〜を調べる

□ **Cherbourg** 名 シェルブール《フランスの地名》

□ **Chernobyl Nuclear Power Plant** チェルノブイリ原子力発電所《ウクライナ (旧:ソビエト連邦) のプ

リピャチ市にあった原子力発電所》

□ **chief** 名 頭, 長

□ **childhood** 名 幼年 [子ども] 時代

□ **China** 名 中国《国名》

□ **chocolate** 名 チョコレート

□ **choice** 名 選択 (の範囲・自由), えり好み, 選ばれた人 [物] **have no choice but to** 〜するしかない

□ **Christian** 名 キリスト教徒, クリスチャン 形 キリスト (教) の

□ **Christianity** 名 キリスト教, キリスト教信仰

□ **Christmas** 名 クリスマス

□ **Church of England** 英国国教会

□ **circle** 名 円, 円形

□ **citizen** 名 ①市民, 国民 ②住民, 民間人

□ **civil** 形 ①一般人の, 民間 (人) の ②国内の, 国家の ③礼儀正しい **civil rights** 公民権 **Civil War** アメリカ南北戦争《1861–65》 **Russian Civil War** ロシア内戦《1917年から1922年にかけて旧ロシア帝国領で争われた内戦》

□ **civilization** 名 文明, 文明人 (化)

□ **claim** 動 主張する

□ **classic** 形 古典的な, 伝統的な 名 古典

□ **clear** 形 はっきりした, 明白な

□ **clever** 形 頭のよい, 利口な

□ **climbing** 名 登ること, 登山

□ **Clint Hill** クリント・ヒル《シークレットサービス, 1932–》

□ **clock** 熟 **around the clock** 24時間体制で

□ **closet** 名 戸棚, 物置, 押し入れ

□ **clothing line** 洋服の型

□ **cloud of smoke** もうもうとした煙

□ **Clyde Barrow** クライド・バロウ

Word List

《1909–1934》

☐ **coast** 名 海岸, 沿岸

☐ **Coast Guard ship** 沿岸警備艇

☐ **Cobh** 名 コーヴ《アイルランドの港町, 当時の名称はクイーンズタウン》

☐ **code** 名 コード, 番号 **Morse code** モールス信号

☐ **collapse** 名 崩壊, 倒壊 動 崩壊する, 崩れる, 失敗する

☐ **colored** 動 color (色をつける) の過去, 過去分詞 形 ①色のついた ②有色人種の, 黒人の

☐ **Columbia University** コロンビア大学

☐ **Columbus** 名《Christopher ～》コロンブス《イタリアの探検家・航海者, 1451–1506》

☐ **combat** 名 戦闘 動 戦う, 効果がある

☐ **come** 熟 come down 下がる come in 中にはいる, やってくる, 出回る come into contact with ～ と接触する, ～に出くわす come out 出てくる, 姿を現す, 発行される come out of ～から出てくる, ～をうまく乗り越える come out with (計画を) 打ち出す come to an end 終わる come up with ～を思いつく, 考え出す

☐ **coming** 動 come (来る) の現在分詞 形 今度の, 来たるべき 名 到来, 来ること

☐ **command** 名 命令, 指揮 (権)

☐ **command module** 司令船《アポロ宇宙船の一部。アポロ宇宙船は司令船, 機械船の2つで構成され, 司令船は飛行士が滞在し, 宇宙船を操縦し地球に帰還させるために必要なすべての制御装置が搭載されている》

☐ **commit** 動 ①委託する ②引き受ける ③(罪などを) 犯す

☐ **commonly** 副 一般に, 通例

☐ **communicate** 動 知らせる, 連絡する

☐ **commute** 動 通勤する, 通学する 名 通学, 通勤

☐ **complement** 動 ①補足する ②よく合わせる 名 補足 (物), 補充

☐ **complete** 形 完全な, まったくの, 完成した 動 完成させる

☐ **component** 名 構成要素, 部品, 成分

☐ **concentrated** 動 concentrate (一点に集める) の過去, 過去分詞 形 ①集中した ②凝縮された, 高濃度の, 濃厚な

☐ **concerned** 動 concern (関係する) の過去, 過去分詞 形 ①関係している, 当事者の ②心配そうな, 気にしている

☐ **concerned about** 《be ～》～について心配している

☐ **condition** 名 ①(健康) 状態, 境遇 ②《-s》状況, 様子

☐ **conduct** 動 実施する, 処理 [処置] する

☐ **conflict** 名 ①不一致, 衝突 ②争い, 対立 ③論争 動 衝突する, 矛盾する

☐ **confrontation** 名 対立, 直面

☐ **confused** 動 confuse (混同する) の過去, 過去分詞 形 困惑した, 混乱した

☐ **confusion** 名 混乱 (状態)

☐ **congress** 名 ①会議, 大会 ②《C-》(米国などの) 国会, 議会 ③協会

☐ **connected** 動 connect (つながる) の過去, 過去分詞 形 結合した, 関係のある

☐ **conquer** 動 征服する, 制圧する

☐ **consciousness** 名 意識, 自覚, 気づいていること

☐ **conservative** 形 ①保守的な ②控えめな, 地味な

☐ **consider** 動 ①考慮する, ～しようと思う ②(～と) みなす ③気にかける, 思いやる

☐ **consist** 動 ①《～ of ～》(部分・要

素から) 成る ②《 – in ～》～に存在する、～にある

□ **constitution** 名①憲法, 規約 ②構成, 構造

□ **contact** 熟come into contact with ～と接触する, ～に出くわす

□ **contain** 動①含む, 入っている ②(感情などを) 抑える

□ **contest** 名(～を目指す) 競争, 競技 動反論する, 争う

□ **context** 名文脈, 前後関係, コンテクスト

□ **continent** 名①大陸, 陸地 ②《the C-》ヨーロッパ大陸

□ **contribute** 動①貢献する ②寄稿する ③寄付する

□ **control** 名①管理, 支配(力) ②抑制 熟get ～ under control ～を制御する, 鎮める take control of ～を制御[管理]する, 支配する

□ **conventional** 形習慣的な

□ **cooling tower** 冷却塔

□ **cooperation** 名①協力, 協業, 協調 ②協同組合

□ **co-pilot** 名副操縦士

□ **copy** 名(書籍の) 一部, 冊

□ **coronavirus** 名《医》コロナウイルス

□ **correct** 形正しい

□ **Cosmopolitan (magazine)** コスモポリタン《雑誌》

□ **cost** 動(金・費用が) かかる, (人に金額を) 費やさせる

□ **could have done** ～だったかもしれない

□ **couple** 名①2つ, 対 ②夫婦, 一組

□ **course** 熟of course もちろん, 当然

□ **court** 名①宮廷, 宮殿 ②法廷, 裁判所

□ **cover** 動覆う, 包む, 隠す

□ **COVID-19** 略新型コロナウイルス

感染症 (= coronavirus disease 2019)

□ **crash** 動 (人・乗り物が) 衝突する, 墜落する 名激突, 墜落

□ **crazy** 形狂気の

□ **create** 動創造する, 生み出す, 引き起こす

□ **creation** 名創造[物]

□ **creative** 形創造力のある, 独創的な

□ **crew** 名クルー, 乗組員, 搭乗員

□ **crib** 名ベビーベッド

□ **crime** 名 (法律上の) 罪, 犯罪

□ **criminal** 形犯罪の, 罪深い, 恥ずべき 名犯罪者, 犯人

□ **criticize** 動①非難する, あら探しをする ②酷評する ③批評する

□ **crowd** 動群がる, 混雑する 名群集, 雑踏, 多数, 聴衆

□ **crowded** 形混雑した, 満員の

□ **crown** 名①冠 ②《the –》王位 ③頂, 頂上 動戴冠する[させる]

□ **cruel** 形残酷な, 厳しい

□ **cruelly** 副残酷に

□ **cruise ship** クルーズ船

□ **crumble** 動粉々になる[する], 崩れる, 砕く

□ **crusader** 名十字軍兵士

□ **crush** 形打ちひしがれて

□ **cry out** 叫ぶ

□ **cultivate** 動耕す, 栽培する, (才能などを) 養う, 育成する

□ **cure** 名治療, 治癒, 矯正 動治療する, 矯正する, 取り除く

□ **curiosity** 名①好奇心 ②珍しい物[存在]

□ **curious** 形好奇心の強い, 珍しい, 奇妙な, 知りたがる

□ **current** 形現在の, 目下の, 通用[流通] している 名流れ, 電流, 風潮

□ **cut off** 切断する, 切り離す

□ **cycle** 图 ①周期, 循環 ②自転車, オートバイ 動 ①循環する ②自転車に乗る

D

□ **Dakota, The** ダコタ・ハウス《ニューヨーク市マンハッタン区にある, 高級集合住宅》

□ **Dallas** 图 ダラス《アメリカ合衆国テキサス州北部にある都市》

□ **Dallas Love Field airport** ダラス・ラブフィールド空港

□ **damage** 图 損害, 損傷 動 損害を与える, 損なう

□ **dangerously** 副 危険なまでに

□ **daring** 形 勇敢な, 大胆な

□ **data** 图 データ, 情報

□ **David Geffen** デヴィッド・ゲフィン《アメリカのレコード会社経営者, 映画プロデューサー, 1943-》

□ **day** 图 in those days あのころは, 当時は

□ **deadliest** 形 deadly (致命的な) の最上級

□ **deal** 動 ①分配する ②《 – with [in] ~》~を扱う 图 ①取引, 扱い ②(不特定の) 量, 額 a good [great] deal (of ~) かなり [ずいぶん・大量] (の ~), 多額 (の~)

□ **Dealey Plaza** ディーリー・プラザ《ダラスの郡庁舎前にある広場》

□ **dearly** 副 とても, 心から

□ **death** 图 ①死, 死ぬこと ②《the – 》終えん, 消滅 be put to death 処刑される Black Death 黒死病 deathe toll 死亡者数 to death 死ぬまで, 死ぬほど

□ **debate** 動 ①討論する ②思案する 图 討論, ディベート

□ **Decameron** 图《the – 》デカメロン《イタリアの作家ボッカチオによる物語集》

□ **decision** 图 決定, 決心

□ **Declaration of Independence** 《the – 》アメリカ独立宣言 (書)

□ **declare** 動 宣言する declare a state of emergency 非常事態宣言をする

□ **decline** 動 ①断る ②傾く ③衰える 图 ①傾くこと ②下り坂, 衰え, 衰退

□ **decrease** 動 減少する 图 減少

□ **dedicated to** ~にささげられる

□ **deem** 動 (~であると) 考える

□ **deeply** 副 深く, 非常に

□ **deep-rooted** 形 根深い

□ **defend** 動 防ぐ, 守る, 弁護する

□ **defense** 图 ①防御, 守備 ②国防

□ **delighted** 形 喜んでいる, うれしそうな

□ **demand** 動 ①要求する, 尋ねる ②必要とする 图 ①要求, 請求 ②需要

□ **Democrat** 图 民主党員

□ **Democratic Party** 《the – 》〈米〉民主党

□ **Department of Defense** 国防総省

□ **depiction** 图 描写, 表現, 叙述

□ **depository** 图 倉庫

□ **depression** 图 不景気, 不況

□ **descent** 图 下り坂, 下降

□ **describe** 動 (言葉で) 描写する, 特色を述べる, 説明する

□ **design** 動 設計する

□ **desperate** 形 ①絶望的な, 見込みのない ②ほしくてたまらない, 必死の

□ **despite** 前 ~にもかかわらず

□ **destination** 图 行き先, 目的地

□ **destroy** 動 破壊する, 絶滅させる, 無効にする

A
B
C
D
E
F
G
H
I
J
K
L
M
N
O
P
Q
R
S
T
U
V
W
X
Y
Z

□ **detail** 图 ①細部,《-s》詳細 ②《-s》個人情報

□ **determine** 動 ①決心する[させる] ②決定する[させる] ③測定する

□ **devastating** 動 devastate（荒らす）の現在分詞 形 破壊的な, 打ちひしぐ, 痛烈な

□ **develop** 動 ①発達する[させる] ②開発する

□ **development** 图 ①発達, 発展 ②開発

□ **devote** 動（～を…に）捧げる

□ **devoted** 形 献身的な, 熱心な, 愛情深い

□ **Diana Spencer** ダイアナ・スペンサー《ウェールズ公妃ダイアナの旧姓》

□ **Diana, Princess of Wales** ウェールズ公妃ダイアナ《ウェールズ公チャールズの最初の妃, 1961-1997》

□ **difficulty** 图 ①むずかしさ ②難局, 支障

□ **dioxide** 图 二酸化物

□ **direct** 形 まっすぐな, 直接の, 率直な

□ **directed at**《be-》～をターゲットにする

□ **directly** 副 ①じかに ②まっすぐに ③ちょうど

□ **disagree** 動 異議を唱える, 反対する

□ **disappear** 動 見えなくなる, 姿を消す, なくなる **disappear into thin air** 虚空に消える

□ **disaster** 图 災害, 災難, まったくの失敗

□ **discharge** 動 ①解き放つ, 解放する ②解雇する ③荷揚げする,（乗客を）降ろす 图 ①解放, 免除 ②荷揚げ ③発砲, 発射

□ **discourage** 動 ①やる気をそぐ, 失望させる ②（～するのを）阻止する, やめさせる

□ **discrimination** 图 差別, 区別, 識別

□ **disease** 图 病気

□ **dissatisfied** 動 dissatisfy（不満を抱かせる）の過去, 過去分詞 形 不満な, 不満そうな

□ **distance** 图 距離, 隔たり, 遠方

□ **distinguished from**《be-》～と区別される

□ **distortion** 图 歪曲, ゆがめること

□ **distract** 動（注意などを）そらす, まぎらす

□ **diverse** 形 ①種々の, 多様な ②異なった

□ **diversity** 图 多様性, 相違

□ **divide** 動 分かれる, 分ける, 割れる, 割る

□ **division** 图 ①分割 ②部門 ③境界 ④割り算

□ **divorce** 動 離婚する 图 離婚, 分離 **file for divorce from**（人）との離婚届を出す

□ **do** 熟 **do well** 成績が良い, 成功する

□ **dock** 图 ドック, 造船所, 波止場, 埠頭

□ **Dodi Fayed** ドディ・（アル）ファイド《エジプトの億万長者モハメド・アルファイドの息子, 映画プロデューサー, 1955-1997》

□ **doing** 图 ①すること, したこと ②《-s》行為, 出来事

□ **Dojo** 图 ドージョー《テスラ社によるニューラルネットワークの学習用スーパーコンピューター》

□ **dominate** 動 支配する, 統治する, 優位を占める

□ **Double Fantasy** ダブル・ファンタジー《ジョン・レノン＆オノ・ヨーコのアルバム, 1980》

□ **down** 熟 **pass down**（次の世代に）伝える

□ **downtown** 形 商業地区[繁華街]の 图 街の中心, 繁華街

□ **dozen** 名 1ダース, 12（個）

□ **drastically** 副 大々的に, 徹底的に, 抜本的に, 急激に

□ **drive off the road** 道から外れて運転する

□ **drive someone out** （人）を追い払う

□ **driven** 動 drive（車で行く）の過去分詞

□ **driving** 動 drive（車で行く）の現在分詞 名 運転

□ **drove** 動 drive（車で行く）の過去

□ **due to** ～によって, ～が原因で

□ **duty** 名 職務, 任務

□ **dynasty** 名 王朝［王家］（の統治期間）

E

□ **each** 熟 each other お互いに each time ～するたびに

□ **earn** 動 儲ける, 稼ぐ

□ **earthquake** 名 地震, 大変動

□ **eastern** 形 ①東方の, 東向きの ②東洋の, 東洋風の

□ **Eastern Europe** 東欧, 東ヨーロッパ

□ **Eastham Prison** イースタム刑務所

□ **eat out** 外食する

□ **economic** 形 経済学の, 経済上の

□ **economically** 副 経済的に, 節約して

□ **economy** 名 ①経済, 財政 ②節約

□ **editor** 名 編集者, 編集長

□ **Edward VIII** エドワード8世《イギリス王, 在位1936》

□ **effect** 名 影響, 効果

□ **effective** 形 効果的である, 有効である

□ **effort** 名 努力（の成果）

□ **either A or B** AかそれともB

□ **elect** 動 選ぶ, （～することに）決める, 選挙する 形 選ばれた

□ **election** 名 選挙, 投票

□ **electric chair** 電気椅子

□ **electric vehicle** 電気自動車, 電動の乗り物（＝EV）

□ **electricity** 名 電気

□ **Elephant Man** エレファント・マン《ジョゼフ・メリックの異名, 1862–1890》

□ **eliminate** 動 削除［排除・除去］する, 撤廃する

□ **elimination** 名 削除, 除外, 撤廃

□ **Elizabeth** 名 エリザベス1世《イングランドとアイルランドの女王, 在位 1558–1603》

□ **elsewhere** 副 どこかほかの所で［へ］

□ **embed** 動 ①〔物を〕埋め込む, 組み込む ②〔～を〕心［記憶］に深く留める

□ **emblem** 名 ①象徴, 標章 ②記章, バッジ

□ **emergence** 名 出現, 参入

□ **emergency** 名 非常時, 緊急時 state of emergency 非常事態 形 緊急の

□ **empire** 名 帝国

□ **encourage** 動 ①勇気づける ②促進する, 助長する

□ **end** 熟 come to an end 終わる in the end とうとう, 結局, ついに

□ **energy cell** 燃料電池

□ **engage in** ～に従事する, 携わる

□ **England** 名 ①イングランド ②英国

□ **entire** 形 全体の, 完全な, まったくの

□ **envelope** 名 封筒, 包み

- □ **equal** 形等しい, 均等な, 平等な
- □ **equality** 名平等, 等しいこと
- □ **era** 名時代, 年代
- □ **escape** 動逃げる, 免れる, もれる 名逃亡, 脱出, もれ
- □ **establish** 動確立する, 立証する, 設置[設立]する
- □ **Eurasia** 名ユーラシア(大陸)《アジアとヨーロッパ全体の大陸》
- □ **Eurasian continent** ユーラシア大陸
- □ **Europe** 名ヨーロッパ
- □ **European** 名ヨーロッパ人 形ヨーロッパ(人)の
- □ **even though** ～にもかかわらず
- □ **ever more** これまで以上に
- □ **every time** ～するときはいつも
- □ **everybody** 代誰でも, 皆
- □ **everyone** 代誰でも, 皆
- □ **everything** 代すべてのこと[もの], 何でも, 何もかも
- □ **evidence** 名①証拠, 証人 ②形跡
- □ **examine** 動試験する, 調査[検査]する, 診察する
- □ **except** 前～を除いて, ～のほかは **except for** ～を除いて, ～がなければ 接～ということを除いて
- □ **excited** 形興奮した, わくわくした
- □ **exclude** 動①排除する, 除く ②(～の)余地を与えない, 考慮しない
- □ **execute** 動処刑する
- □ **execution** 名処刑
- □ **exemplify** 動①(～の)良い[典型的な]例となる ②(～の)実例を挙げる
- □ **exhausted** 動exhaust(ひどく疲れさせる)の過去, 過去分詞 形疲れ切った, 消耗した
- □ **exhaustion** 名①極度の疲労 ②消耗, 使い果たすこと

- □ **exist** 動存在する, 生存する, ある, いる
- □ **expand** 動①広げる, 拡張[拡大]する ②発展させる, 拡充する
- □ **expect** 動予期[予測]する, (当然のこととして)期待する
- □ **experiment** 名実験, 試み 動実験する, 試みる
- □ **expert** 名専門家, 熟練者, エキスパート 形熟練した, 専門の
- □ **explode** 動①爆発する[させる] ②(感情が)ほとばしる, 突然～し出す
- □ **exploration** 名探検, 実地調査
- □ **explorer** 名探検者[家]
- □ **exterminate** 動絶滅させる, 根絶する
- □ **extra** 形余分の, 臨時の
- □ **extremely** 副非常に, 極度に

F

- □ **facility** 名《-ties》施設, 設備
- □ **fact** 熟 **as a matter of fact** 実際は, 実のところ **in fact** つまり, 実は
- □ **fail** 動①失敗する, 落第する[させる] ②《-to ～》～し損なう, ～できない ③失望させる 名失敗, 落第点
- □ **failure** 名①失敗, 落第 ②不足, 欠乏
- □ **faith** 名①信念, 信仰 ②信頼, 信用
- □ **fall down** 落ちる, 転ぶ
- □ **fall to the ground** 転ぶ
- □ **fallen** 動fall(落ちる)の過去分詞
- □ **false** 形うその, 間違った, にせの, 不誠実な 副不誠実に
- □ **family line** 家系
- □ **famous for** 《be -》～で有名である
- □ **fantasy** 名空想, 夢想

132

□ **fate** 名 ①運命, 宿命 ②破滅, 悲運

□ **FBI** 略《米》連邦捜査局 (= Federal Bureau of Investigation)

□ **fear** 名 ①恐れ ②心配, 不安 動 ① 恐れる ②心配する

□ **federal** 形 連邦政府の, 連邦の

□ **feeling** 名 感じ, 気持ち

□ **fellow** 名 仲間, 同僚

□ **female** 形 女性の

□ **feudal** 形 封建制度の, 封建的な

□ **feudal lord** 〔中世の〕(封建) 領主

□ **fiction** 名 フィクション, 作り話, 小説

□ **fierce** 形 どう猛な, 荒々しい, すさまじい, 猛烈な

□ **fight back** 反撃に転じる, 応戦する

□ **fighting** 名 戦闘

□ **figure** 名 人〔物〕の姿, 形 動 **figure out** 理解する, ~であるとわかる, (原因などを) 解明する

□ **file** 動 (書類などを) 提出する **file for divorce from** (人) との離婚届を出す

□ **final** 形 最後の, 決定的な

□ **finance** 名 ①財政, 財務 ②(銀行からの) 資金, 融資 ③《 – s》財政状態, 財源 動 資金を融通する

□ **financial** 形 ①財務 (上) の, 金融 (上) の ②金融関係者の

□ **financial resource** 金融資産, 財源

□ **find out** 見つけ出す, 気がつく, 知る, 調べる, 解明する

□ **fingerprint** 名 指紋

□ **fire** 熟 **catch on fire** 燃えだす

□ **firefighter** 名 消防士

□ **firmly** 副 しっかりと, 断固として

□ **first** 熟 **at first sight** 一目見て **first of all** まず第一に

□ **Fishtrap Cemetery** フィッシュ

トラップ墓地

□ **fit** 動 合致 [適合] する, 合致させる

□ **fix** 動 修理する

□ **flat** 形 平らな

□ **flea** 名 ノミ (蚤)

□ **fled** 動 flee (逃げる) の過去, 過去分詞

□ **flight** 名 飛ぶこと, 飛行, (飛行機の) フライト

□ **flood** 動 あふれさせる, 水浸しにする

□ **Florida** 名 フロリダ州

□ **flow** 動 流れ出る, 流れる, あふれる 名 ①流出 ②流ちょう (なこと)

□ **flu** 名 インフルエンザ, 流感

□ **fly out of** ~から飛び立つ

□ **flying** 名 飛行 形 飛んでいる, 空中に浮かぶ, (飛ぶように) 速い

□ **focus** 名 ①焦点, ピント ②関心の的, 着眼点 ③中心 動 ①焦点を合わせる ②(関心・注意を) 集中させる

□ **followed by** その後に~が続いて

□ **following** 形《the – 》次の, 次に続く

□ **for ~ years** ~年間, ~年にわたって

□ **force** 名 力, 勢い 動 強制する, 力ずくで~する, 余儀なく~させる

□ **Ford's Theatre** フォード劇場《ワシントンD.C.にある劇場》

□ **forehead** 名 ひたい

□ **form** 名 形, 形式 **take the form of** ~となって現れる

□ **formally** 副 ①正式に, 公式に ②形式的に ③儀式ばって, 堅苦しく

□ **former** 形 ①前の, 先の, 以前の ②《the – 》(二者のうち) 前者の

□ **forward** 副 前方に

□ **foster** 動 ①育てる, 促進させる ②心に抱く 形 里親の

□ **foundation** 名 ①建設, 創設 ②

基礎, 土台

- □ **France** 名 フランス《国名》
- □ **Francis I** フランツ1世《神聖ロー マ皇帝, 1708–1765》
- □ **Frank Hamer** フランク・ヘイマ ー《テキサス・レンジャー(テキサス 州警備隊の隊員), 1884–1955》
- □ **Frankish** 形 フランク族[語]の 名 フランク語
- □ **Frankish kingdom** フランク 王国《5世紀後半にゲルマン人の部族, フランク人によって建てられた王国》
- □ **freak** 名 変人, 熱狂的ファン, 奇形
- □ **freak show** 見世物《奇形の動物 や人を見せる》
- □ **Fred Haise, Jr.** フレッド・ヘイ ズ《アメリカ航空宇宙局(NASA)の 宇宙飛行士, 1933–》
- □ **Fred Noonan** フレッド・ヌーナ ン《フライト・ナビゲータ, 1893– 1937》
- □ **Frederick Treves** フレデリッ ク・トレヴェス《外科医, 1853–1923》
- □ **free** 熟 set free (人)を解放する, 釈 放される, 自由の身になる
- □ **freedom** 名 ①自由 ②束縛がない こと
- □ **French** 形 フランス(人・語)の 名 ①フランス語 ②《the –》フラン ス人
- □ **French Revolution** フランス革 命《18世紀にフランスで起きた市民 革命》
- □ **frequently** 副 頻繁に, しばしば
- □ **from ～ to ...** ～から…まで
- □ **fruition** 名 ①〔望んだものの〕達成, 成就 ②〔望んだ結果が得られた〕達 成感 ③《植物》結実, 実を結ぶこと
- □ **frustrated** 動 frustrate (挫折させ る)の過去・過去分詞 形 挫折した, 失 望した
- □ **Fukushima Daiichi** 福島第一 原子力発電所

- □ **full of** 《be –》～で一杯である
- □ **full-blown** 形 ①〔花が〕満開の ②成熟した ③万全の, 本格的な
- □ **full-on** 形 徹底した
- □ **full-scale** 形 全面的な
- □ **fully** 副 十分に, 完全に, まるまる
- □ **fun** 熟 for fun 楽しみで make fun of ～を物笑いの種にする, からかう
- □ **function** 動 働く, 機能する 名 機 能, 作用
- □ **fund** 名 ①資金, 基金, 財源 ②金 ③公債, 国債 動 ①資金を出す ②長 期公債の借り換えをする
- □ **fundamental** 名 基本, 原理 形 基本の, 根本的な, 重要な
- □ **funeral** 名 葬式, 葬列 funeral procession 葬列 形 葬式の
- □ **funny** 形 ①おもしろい, こっけい な ②奇妙な, うさんくさい
- □ **further** 形 いっそう遠い, その上の, なおいっそうの 副 いっそう遠く, そ の上に, もっと 動 促進する
- □ **future** 熟 in the future 将来は

G

- □ **gain** 動 ①得る, 増す ②進歩する, 進む
- □ **gambling** 名 賭博
- □ **gap** 名 ギャップ, 隔たり, すき間 動 すき間ができる
- □ **gas** 名 ガス, 気体
- □ **gasoline-powered** 形 ガソリ ン動力の
- □ **gather** 動 集まる, 集める
- □ **Geffen Records** ゲフィン・レコ ード《アメリカ合衆国のレコード・レ ーベル》
- □ **general** 形 一般の, 普通の in general 一般に, たいてい
- □ **generally** 副 ①一般に, だいたい

②たいてい **generally speaking** 一般的に言えば

□ **generation** 名①同世代の人々 ②一世代 ③発生, 生成

□ **George Floyd** ジョージ・フロイド《2020年5月25日, ミネソタ州ミネアポリスで逮捕される最中に警官に死亡させられたアフリカ系アメリカ人》

□ **George V** ジョージ5世《イギリス王, 在位1910-1936》

□ **George W. Bush** ジョージ・W・ブッシュ《第43代アメリカ合衆国大統領, 任期2001-2009》

□ **Georgia** 名ジョージア州《米国フロリダ州のすぐ北 大西洋岸にある州》

□ **German** 形ドイツ(人・語)の 名①ドイツ人 ②ドイツ語

□ **German measles** 風疹, 三日ばしか

□ **Germany** 名ドイツ《国名》

□ **get** 熟**get home** 家に着く[帰る] **get in** 中に入る, 乗り込む **get into a car** 車に乗り込む **get on** (電車などに)乗る **get out of** ~から下車する, ~から取り出す, ~から外へ出る[抜け出る] **get rid of** ~を取り除く **get there** そこに到着する, 目的を達成する, 成功する **get to** ~に達する[到着する] **get** ~ **under control** ~を制御する, 鎮める **get worse** 悪化する

□ **ghost** 名幽霊

□ **give back** (~を)返す

□ **give birth to** ~を生む

□ **give up** あきらめる, やめる, 引き渡す

□ **global** 形地球(上)の, 地球規模の, 世界的な, 国際的な

□ **global warming** 地球温暖化

□ **glory** 名栄光, 名誉, 繁栄

□ **go** 熟**go a long way** 大いに役立つ **go about business as usual** 普段どおりに仕事をする **go around** ~を周回する **go into** ~に入る **go into shock** ショック状態に陥る **go on** 続く, 続ける, 進み続ける, 起こる, 発生する **go through** 通り抜ける, 成立する, 経験する **go up to** ~まで行く, 近づく **go without** ~なしですませる

□ **God** 熟**My God.** おや, まあ

□ **golden** 形①金色の ②金製の ③貴重な

□ **Gone but not forgotten** 「あなたは去った。しかし忘れられることはない」

□ **goodnight** 間《就寝時・夜の別れのあいさつ》おやすみ

□ **gotten** 動get (得る) の過去分詞

□ **government** 名政治, 政府, 支配

□ **governor** 名知事

□ **GP Putnam** ジョージ・P・パットナム《政治評論家, 出版者, 1887-1950》

□ **Grace Muriel Earhart** グレイス・ミュリエル・イアハート《アメリア・イアハートの妹, 1899-1998》

□ **gradually** 副だんだんと

□ **grand** 形雄大な, 壮麗な

□ **grandson** 名孫息子, 男の孫

□ **grave** 名墓

□ **Great Britain** 英国, イギリス

□ **Great Depression** 世界恐慌《1929年10月24日にニューヨーク証券取引所で株価が大暴落したことを端緒として世界的な規模で各国の経済に波及した金融恐慌, および経済後退》

□ **Greek** 形ギリシア(人・語)の 名①ギリシア人 ②ギリシア語

□ **greet** 動①あいさつする ②(喜んで)迎える

□ **grief** 名(深い)悲しみ, 悲嘆

□ **ground** 熟**fall to the ground** 転ぶ **on the ground** 地面に

□ **ground control** 地上管制

□ **growing** 動 grow (成長する) の現在分詞 形 成長期にある, 大きくなりつつある

□ **guarantee** 名 保証, 保証書, 保証人 動 保証する, 請け合う

□ **guard** 名 ①警戒, 見張り ②番人 動 番をする, 監視する, 守る

□ **guilty** 形 有罪の, やましい

□ **gun** 名 銃

□ **gym** 名 体育館, ジム

H

□ **hail** 動 歓呼して迎える, 歓迎する

□ **Hail to the Chief** 大統領万歳《アメリカ合衆国大統領のための公式アンセム》

□ **halfway** 副 中間 [中途] で, 不完全に 形 中間 [中途] の, 不完全な

□ **hand** 熟 hand in 差し出す, 提出する hand over 手渡す, 引き渡す, 譲渡する on the other hand 一方, 他方では

□ **happen to** たまたま〜する, 偶然〜する

□ **happiness** 名 幸せ, 喜び

□ **hard to** 〜し難い

□ **harden** 動 固める, 固くする, 頑固にする

□ **harmony** 名 調和, 一致, ハーモニー

□ **Harry Manning** ハリー・マニング《海軍大尉, 1897–1974》

□ **harsh** 形 厳しい, とげとげしい, 不快な

□ **hate** 名 憎しみ

□ **have** 熟 could have done 〜だったかもしれない have no choice but to 〜するしかない

□ **Hawaii** 名 ハワイ《米国の州》

□ **head for** 〜に向かう, 〜の方に進む

□ **head-to-head** 副 接戦で, わずかの差で 形 ①接近戦の, 接戦の ②直接対決の, 1 対 1 の

□ **healthy** 形 健康な, 健全な, 健康によい

□ **heart** 熟 by heart 暗記して heart attack 心臓麻痺

□ **heat** 名 熱, 暑さ

□ **heating system** 暖房装置

□ **heavily** 副 ①重く, 重そうに, ひどく ②多量に

□ **hegemony** 名 ①覇権, ヘゲモニー ②〔ヘゲモニーを持つ〕覇権国家

□ **height** 名 高さ

□ **heir** 名 相続人, 後継者

□ **helper** 名 助手, 助けになるもの

□ **Henry** 名 ヘンリー(・オブ・ウェールズ王子)《ウェールズ公チャールズとダイアナ妃の次男, 現サセックス公爵, 1984–》

□ **Henry VIII** ヘンリー8世《イングランド王, 在位 1509–1547》

□ **here is 〜** こちらは〜です

□ **heretic** 名 《カトリック》異端者

□ **heritage** 名 遺産, 相続財産

□ **hid** 動 hide (隠れる) の過去, 過去分詞

□ **hidden** 動 hide (隠れる) の過去分詞 形 隠れた, 秘密の

□ **hiding** 熟 in hiding 隠れている

□ **highly** 副 ①大いに, 非常に ②高度に, 高位に ③高く評価して, 高価で

□ **high-positioned** 形 高い身分の

□ **hijack** 動 ハイジャックする, 乗っ取る

□ **historic** 形 歴史上有名 [重要] な, 歴史的な

□ **hold on** しっかりつかまる

- □ **holy** 形 聖なる, 神聖な
- □ **Holy Roman Empire** 神聖ローマ帝国《現在のドイツ, オーストリア, チェコ, イタリア北部を中心に存在していた国家, 800/962-1806》
- □ **home** 熟 **get home** 家に着く[帰る]
- □ **home appliances** 家電機器[製品]
- □ **Honolulu** 名 ホノルル《ハワイ州の都市》
- □ **horrific** 形 〔物事の性質が〕恐ろしい, ゾッとするような
- □ **House of Representatives** 〔米国などの二院制議会の〕下院
- □ **housing** 名 住宅供給, 住居, 家
- □ **Houston** 名 ヒューストン
- □ **however** 接 けれども, だが
- □ **Howland Island** ハウランド島《北太平洋にあるアメリカ領の無人島》
- □ **huge** 形 巨大な, ばく大な
- □ **human race** 人類
- □ **humankind** 名 (種としての)人類, 人間
- □ **Hundred Years War** 《the – 》百年戦争《フランスのヴァロワ家とイギリスのプランタジネット家の間で, 1337年から1453年にわたって行われた一連の戦争》
- □ **Hungary** 名 ハンガリー《国名》
- □ **hunt** 名 狩り, 追跡
- □ **hunting** 名 狩り, 狩猟, ハンティング

I

- □ **I do not mean to** ～するつもりはないのですが
- □ **Iberian Peninsula** イベリア半島《ヨーロッパの南西》

- □ **iceberg** 名 氷山
- □ **ideal** 名 理想, 究極の目標 形 理想的な, 申し分のない
- □ **identify** 動 (本人・同一と)確認する, 見分ける
- □ **if** 熟 **as if** あたかも～のように, まるで～みたいに **if any** もしあれば, あったとしても **see if** ～かどうかを確かめる
- □ **ignorance** 名 無知, 無学
- □ **Illinois** 名 イリノイ州
- □ **illness** 名 病気
- □ **image** 名 ①印象, 姿 ②画像, 映像
- □ **imagine** 動 想像する, 心に思い描く
- □ **immediately** 副 すぐに, ～するやいなや
- □ **immigrant** 名 移民, 移住者
- □ **impact** 名 影響力, 反響, 効果 動 ①詰め込む ②衝突する
- □ **import** 動 輸入する 名 輸入, 輸入品
- □ **imprison** 動 投獄する, 閉じ込める
- □ **improve** 動 改善する[させる], 進歩する
- □ **incident** 名 出来事, 事故, 事変, 紛争 形 ①起こりがちな ②付随する
- □ **incite** 動 〔人や感情を〕あおり立てる, 奮い立たせる
- □ **include** 動 含む, 勘定に入れる
- □ **including** 前 ～を含めて, 込みで
- □ **incorporate** 動 ①合体させる ②法人組織にする
- □ **increase** 動 増加[増強]する, 増やす, 増える 名 増加(量), 増大
- □ **independence** 名 独立心, 自立
- □ **independent** 形 独立した, 自立した
- □ **in the blink of an eye** 瞬く間に, あっという間に

□ **indicate** 動①指す, 示す, (道など を) 教える ②それとなく言う ③きざ しがある

□ **indicator** 名指標, 指針

□ **individual** 形独立した, 個性的な, 個々の 名個体, 個人

□ **industrial** 形工業の, 産業の

□ **Industrial Revolution** 産業革命

□ **industry** 名産業, 工業

□ **inequality** 名①不平等, 不均衡 ②《-ties》起伏, (表面の) 荒いこと ③ (天候・温度の) 変動 ④不等式

□ **inevitable** 形避けられない, 必然的な

□ **infantry** 名歩兵

□ **infect** 動①感染する, 伝染する ② (病気を) 移す ③影響を及ぼす

□ **infection** 名 (病気など) 感染, 伝染

□ **infectious** 形伝染性の, うつりやすい

□ **infidel** 名不信心者, 異端者 形宗教心のない, 不信心な

□ **inform** 動告げる, 知らせる

□ **infrastructure** 名①基礎 [下部] 構造 ②〔社会の〕基盤, インフラ

□ **inheritance** 名①相続 (財産), 遺産 ②遺伝

□ **injure** 動痛める, 傷つける

□ **innovation** 名①革新, 刷新 ②新しいもの, 新考案

□ **input** 動入力する 名入力, 投入

□ **inspiration** 名霊感, ひらめき, 妙案, 吸気

□ **instant** 形即時の, 緊急の, 即席の

□ **instantly** 副すぐに, 即座に

□ **instead** 副その代わりに **instead of** ~の代わりに, ~をしないで

□ **instigate** 動①〔~を〕引き起こす, 駆り立てる ②〔人を悪い方向へ〕そそのかす, 扇動する

□ **institute** 動①制定する ② (調査を) 実施する 名協会, 研究所

□ **institution** 名機関, 施設, 団体

□ **instruction** 名教えること, 指示, 助言

□ **insurance** 名保険

□ **integrate** 動①統合する, 一体化する ②溶け込ませる, 溶け込む, 差別をなくす

□ **intellectual** 形知的な, 知性のある 名知識人, 有識者

□ **intellectual activity** 知的活動

□ **intelligence** 名①知能 ②情報

□ **intend** 動《 – to ~》~しようと思う, ~するつもりである

□ **interested** 形興味を持った, 関心のある **be interested in** ~に興味 [関心] がある

□ **interesting** 動 interest (興味を起こさせる) の現在分詞 形おもしろい, 興味を起こさせる

□ **internal bleeding** 内出血

□ **internal organ** 内臓器官

□ **International Group for Historic Aircraft Recovery, The** タイガー《航空機の捜索や保存を行っている研究グループ, 略称 TIGHAR》

□ **international politics** 国際政治

□ **intruder** 名侵入者, 妨害者

□ **invade** 動侵入する, 攻め入る

□ **invasion** 名侵略, 侵害

□ **invent** 動①発明 [考案] する ②ねつ造する

□ **investigation** 名 (徹底的な) 調査, 取り調べ

□ **investor** 名①出資者, 投資家 ②授与者

□ **invisible** 名目に見えないもの 形目に見えない, 表に出ない

□ **involved** 動 involve (含む) の過去,

過去分詞 形 ①巻き込まれている，関連する ②入り組んだ，込み入っている

- **iPhone** 名 アイフォーン《アップル社製のスマートフォン》
- **Iraq** 名 イラク《国名》
- **Ireland** 名 アイルランド《国名》
- **ironically** 副 皮肉にも，皮肉なことに
- **Islam** 名 イスラム教［教徒・文化］
- **Islamic** 形 イスラムの，イスラム教の
- **Islamic fundamentalist** イスラム原理主義者
- **Islamist** 形 イスラム教徒［原理主義者］の
- **isolate** 動 隔離する，孤立させる
- **Israel** 名 イスラエル《国名》
- **issue** 名 ①問題，論点 ②発行物 ③出口，流出 動 ①（〜から）出る，生じる ②発行する
- **It takes someone 〜 to ...** （人）が …するのに〜（時間など）がかかる
- **Italy** 名 イタリア《国名》
- **Itasca** 名 イタスカ号《沿岸警備艇の名》
- **itself** 代 それ自体，それ自身
- **I've Been to the Mountaintop** 「私は山頂に達した」《キング牧師が暗殺される前日のスピーチ》

J

- **Jack the Ripper** 切り裂きジャック《1888年にイギリスで連続発生した猟奇殺人事件の犯人の通称》
- **jacket** 名 ①短い上着 ②（書物などの）カバー
- **Jacqueline Kennedy** ジャクリーン・ケネディ《第35代アメリカ合衆国大統領ジョン・F・ケネディの夫人，1929–1994》
- **jail** 名 刑務所
- **James Earl Ray** ジェームズ・アール・レイ《犯罪者，1928–1998》
- **Jane Grey, Lady** レディ・ジェーン・グレイ《イングランドのテューダー朝第4代の女王（在位1553年7月10日–19日），1537–1554》
- **Jane Seymour** ジェーン・シーモア《イングランド王ヘンリー8世の3番目の王妃（1536年結婚）1509–1537》
- **Japan** 名 日本《国名》
- **jaw** 名 ①あご ②（-s）あご状のもの
- **Jerusalem** 名 エルサレム《イスラエルの首都》
- **Jew** 名 ユダヤ人［教徒］
- **jewel** 名 宝石
- **Jim Lovell, Jr.** ジム・ラヴェル《アメリカ航空宇宙局（NASA）の宇宙飛行士，1928–》
- **Joe Biden** ジョー・バイデン《アメリカ合衆国第46代大統領（2021–），1942–》
- **John Condon** ジョン・コンドン《元教師，誘拐事件の仲介役を務めた》
- **John Connally** ジョン・コナリー《テキサス州の政治家，1917–1993》
- **John F. Kennedy** ジョン・F・ケネディ《第35代アメリカ合衆国大統領，任期1961–1963》
- **John Fitzgerald Kennedy** ジョン・フィッツジェラルド・ケネディ《第35代アメリカ合衆国大統領，任期1961–1963》
- **John Lennon** ジョン・レノン《イギリスのミュージシャン。ビートルズのメンバー，1940–1980》
- **John Swigert, Jr.** ジョン・スワイガート《アメリカ航空宇宙局（NASA）の宇宙飛行士，1931–1982》
- **John Wilkes Booth** ジョン・ウィルクス・ブース《アメリカの俳優，

1838–1865》

- □ **Joseph Merrick** ジョゼフ・メリック《「エレファント・マン」として知られた, 1862–1890》
- □ **just as** (ちょうど)であろうとおり
- □ **justice system** 司法制度

K

- □ **Kansas** 名 カンザス州
- □ **Kennedy Space Center** ケネディ宇宙センター《アメリカ合衆国フロリダ州ブレバード郡メリット島にある, アメリカ航空宇宙局(NASA)の有人宇宙船発射場及び打ち上げ管制施設》
- □ **kidnap** 動 誘拐する
- □ **kidnapper** 名 誘拐犯
- □ **kidnapping** 名 誘拐
- □ **killer** 名 殺人者[犯]
- □ **killing** 名 殺害, 殺人 **mass killing** 大量殺人
- □ **kilometer** 名 キロメートル《長さの単位》
- □ **kingdom** 名 王国
- □ **kiss** 動 キスする
- □ **knee** 名 ひざ
- □ **know-how** 名 ノウハウ
- □ **knowledge** 名 知識, 理解, 学問
- □ **known as** 《be –》～として知られている

L

- □ **labor** 名 出産, 分娩
- □ **Lady Diana Spencer** レディ・ダイアナ・スペンサー《ウェールズ公妃ダイアナの旧姓》
- □ **Lady Jane Grey** レディ・ジェーン・グレイ《イングランドのテュー

ダー朝第4代の女王(在位1553年7月10日–19日), 1537–1554》

- □ **Lae** 名 ラエ《パプアニューギニア第2の都市》
- □ **laid** 動 lay (置く)の過去, 過去分詞
- □ **landing** 名 上陸, 着陸
- □ **large number of** 多数の～, 多くの～
- □ **laughter** 名 笑い(声)
- □ **launch** 動 (ロケットなどを)打ち上げる, 発射する
- □ **lay** 動 lie (横たわる)の過去
- □ **Lazaretto Vecchio** ラザレット・ヴェッキオ《イタリアのヴェネツィア本島の南にある小島》
- □ **lead to** ～に至る, ～に通じる, ～を引き起こす
- □ **leadership** 名 指揮, リーダーシップ
- □ **leading** 動 lead (導く)の現在分詞 形 主要な, 指導的な, 先頭の
- □ **leaning** 名 ①傾き, 傾斜 ②〔～を好む〕傾向
- □ **least** 名 最小, 最少 **at least** 少なくとも
- □ **leather** 名 皮革, 皮製品
- □ **Leather Apron** レザーエプロン《「切り裂きジャック」事件の異名。犯人が革のエプロンをしていたとされる》
- □ **leave ～ alone** ～をそっとしておく
- □ **led** 動 lead (導く)の過去, 過去分詞
- □ **Lee Harvey Oswald** リー・ハーヴェイ・オズワルド《アメリカ合衆国第35代大統領ジョン・F・ケネディ暗殺の実行犯とされる, 1939–1963》
- □ **legal** 形 法律(上)の, 正当な
- □ **Leicester** レスター《英国の地名》
- □ **less** 形 ～より小さい[少ない]
- □ **Level 7** レベル7《最悪レベルの原

Word List

子力事故）

- [ ] **liberal** 形 ①自由主義の, 進歩的な ②気前のよい 名 自由主義者
- [ ] **license** 名 許可, 免許証
- [ ] **lie down** 横たわる, 横になる
- [ ] **life in prison** 終身刑
- [ ] **life savings** 老後の蓄え, ためてきたお金
- [ ] **lifeboat** 名 救命ボート
- [ ] **lifestyle** 名 生活様式, ライフスタイル
- [ ] **like** 熟 like never before かつてないほど sound like ～のように聞こえる would like to ～したいと思う
- [ ] **likely** 形 ①ありそうな, (～)しそうな ②適当な 副 たぶん, おそらく
- [ ] **limit** 動 制限［限定］する
- [ ] **line** 熟 line up (位置を)調整する next in line 列の順番が次
- [ ] **lip** 名 唇,《-s》口
- [ ] **living** 名 生計, 生活 形 生活のための
- [ ] **load** 動 (荷を)積む
- [ ] **locate** 動 置く, 居住する［させる］
- [ ] **location** 名 位置, 場所
- [ ] **London** 名 ロンドン《英国の首都》
- [ ] **London Hospital** 王立ロンドン病院
- [ ] **lonely** 形 孤独な, 心さびしい
- [ ] **long** 熟 as long as ～する以上は, ～である限りは
- [ ] **long-time** 形 長年の, 長期にわたる
- [ ] **longer** 熟 no longer もはや～でない［～しない］ not be much longer あまり長く持たない
- [ ] **longevity** 名 長命, 長生き, 寿命
- [ ] **look** 熟 look down on ～を見下す look down upon ～を見下す, 俯瞰する look for ～を探す look into ①～を検討する, ～を研究する ②～

の中を見る, ～をのぞき込む look over ～越しに見る, ～を見渡す look to ～に目をやる

- [ ] **lord** 名 首長, 主人, 領主,《L》(キリスト教の) 神
- [ ] **Lorraine Motel** ロレイン・モーテル《キング牧師のメンフィスにおける常泊先だった。現在は国立公民権博物館として公開されている》
- [ ] **loss** 名 損失(額・物), 損害
- [ ] **loudly** 副 大声で, 騒がしく
- [ ] **Louis Charles** ルイ＝シャルル《フランス国王ルイ16世と王妃マリー・アントワネットの次男。ルイ17世, 1785–1795》
- [ ] **Louis Gordon** ルイス・ゴードン《1928年アメリカ・イアハートが共同パイロットとして大西洋横断したときのチームの副操縦士兼エンジニア, 1901–1964》
- [ ] **Louis Joseph Xavier Francois** ルイ＝ジョゼフ・ド・フランス《ルイ16世と王妃マリー・アントワネットの第2子, 1781–1789》
- [ ] **Louis XVI** ルイ16世《フランス王, 1754–1793》
- [ ] **Louis-Auguste** 名 ルイ＝オーギュスト《フランス王ルイ16世の正式名》
- [ ] **Louisiana** 名 ルイジアナ州
- [ ] **love** 熟 be in love with ～に恋して, ～に心を奪われて
- [ ] **loved one** 最愛の人
- [ ] **lover** 名 ①愛人, 恋人 ②愛好者
- [ ] **low** 熟 run low 残り少なくなる
- [ ] **low-class** 形 下層階級の
- [ ] **lumpy** 形 ①でこぼこの, 塊の多い ②鈍重な, ずんぐりした
- [ ] **lunar** 形 月の, 月面の
- [ ] **lunar module** 月着陸船《アポロ宇宙船》
- [ ] **lying** 動 lie (横たわる) の現在分詞
- [ ] **Lyndon B. Johnson** リンドン・

141

B・ジョンソン《第36代アメリカ合衆国大統領, 任期1963–1969》

M

☐ **Macon** 图 メイコン郡《地名, アラバマ州》

☐ **made public** 《be –》公になる

☐ **madly** 副 ①気が狂って ②猛烈に, すごく

☐ **madness** 狂気, 熱中

☐ **maiden** 形 ①未婚の ②初めての, 処女の

☐ **maiden voyage** 処女航海

☐ **main** 形 主な, 主要な

☐ **maintain** 動 ①維持する ②養う

☐ **major** 形 大きいほうの, 主な

☐ **make a speech** 演説をする

☐ **make fun of** ～を物笑いの種にする, からかう

☐ **make ~ out of …** ～を…から作る

☐ **make sure** 確かめる, 確認する, 必ずする

☐ **make up** 作り出す, 考え出す, ～を構成[形成]する

☐ **manage** 動 ①動かす, うまく処理する ②経営[管理]する, 支配する ③どうにか～する

☐ **manager** 图 経営者, 支配人, 支店長, 部長

☐ **mankind** 图 人類, 人間

☐ **manned** 形 (宇宙船などが) 有人の

☐ **manufacture** 動 製造[製作]する 图 製造, 製作, 製品

☐ **manufacturer** 图 製造業者, メーカー

☐ **many** 熟 so many 非常に多くの

☐ **margin** 图 ①ふち, 余白, 欄外 ②余裕 ③利ざや, マージン

☐ **Maria Theresa** マリア・テレジア《神聖ローマ皇帝フランツ1世の皇后にして共同統治者, 1717–1780》

☐ **Marie Antoinette** マリー・アントワネット《フランス国王ルイ16世の王妃, 1755–1793》

☐ **Mark David Chapman** マーク・デイヴィッド・チャップマン《1955–》

☐ **marriage** 图 結婚 (生活・式)

☐ **marry** 動 結婚する

☐ **Martha's Vineyard** マーサズ・ヴィニヤード《アメリカ, マサチューセッツ州に属する島》

☐ **Martin Luther King, Jr.** マーティン・ルーサー・キング・ジュニア《アメリカ合衆国のプロテスタントバプテスト派の牧師。通称キング牧師。1929–1968》

☐ **Marvin** 图 マーヴィン《クライド・バロウの兄, 1903–1933》

☐ **Mary** 图 マリア (・ニコラエヴナ)《ニコライ2世第三皇女, 1899–1918》

☐ **Mary I** メアリー1世《イングランド女王, 別名ブラッディ・メアリー, 在位1553–1558》

☐ **Mary Todd Lincoln** メアリー・トッド・リンカーン《第16代アメリカ合衆国大統領エイブラハム・リンカーンの妻, 1818–1882》

☐ **mass** 图 多数, 多量 mass killing 大量殺人

☐ **Massachusetts** 图 マサチューセッツ州

☐ **massacre** 图 大虐殺, 皆殺し 動 虐殺する, 殺りくする

☐ **masterpiece** 图 傑作, 名作, 代表作

☐ **material** 图 材料, 原料

☐ **matter** 熟 as a matter of fact 実際は, 実のところ not matter 問題にならない radioactive matter 放射性物質

☐ **mean** 熟 I do not mean to ～する

つもりはないのですが

☐ **measles** 名はしか, 麻疹

☐ **measure** 動①測る, (～の)寸法がある ②評価する 名①寸法, 測定, 計量, 単位 ②程度, 基準

☐ **media** 名メディア, マスコミ, 媒体

☐ **medieval** 形中世の, 中世風の

☐ **Mediterranean** 形地中海(沿岸)の 名《the M-》地中海

☐ **meeting** 名集まり, ミーティング

☐ **melt** 動溶ける

☐ **memorial** 形記念の, 追悼の

☐ **memorize** 動暗記する, 記憶する

☐ **memory** 名記憶(力), 思い出

☐ **Memphis** 名メンフィス(市)《テネシー州》

☐ **mention** 動(～について)述べる, 言及する 名言及, 陳述

☐ **Mercedes** 名メルセデス(・ベンツ)《車名》

☐ **meter** 名メートル《長さの単位》

☐ **Miami** 名マイアミ《フロリダ州の主要都市》

☐ **middle** 名中間, 最中 **in the middle of** ～の真ん中[中ほど]に 形中間の, 中央の

☐ **Middle Ages** 《the – 》中世《西洋史における5世紀から15世紀の時代区分》

☐ **Middle East** 中東

☐ **midnight** 名夜の12時, 真夜中

☐ **midst** 名真ん中, 中央

☐ **might** 動《mayの過去》①～かもしれない ②～してもよい, ～できる

☐ **mile** 名マイル《長さの単位。1,609m》

☐ **military** 形軍隊[軍人]の, 軍事の 名《the – 》軍, 軍部

☐ **mind** 名①心, 精神, 考え ②知性 動①気にする, いやがる ②気をつける, 用心する

☐ **minister** 名①大臣, 閣僚, 公使 ②聖職者

☐ **Minnesota** 名ミネソタ州《米国・中西部にある州》

☐ **mirror** 名鏡

☐ **missing** 形欠けている, 行方不明の 名《the – 》行方不明者

☐ **mission** 名使命, 任務

☐ **mob** 名群集, やじ馬 動群がる, 襲う, 殺到する

☐ **model** 名模型

☐ **Model 3** モデル3《テスラ社が製造・販売しているコンパクト・ラグジュアリーセダンタイプの電気自動車》

☐ **Model Y** モデルY《テスラ社が製造・販売しているコンパクトSUVタイプの電気自動車》

☐ **modern** 形現代[近代]の, 現代的な

☐ **modernization** 名近代[現代]化

☐ **module** 名基準単位, モジュール

☐ **moment** 名①瞬間, ちょっとの間 ②(特定の)時, 時期

☐ **Mongol** 名モンゴル人[語], モンゴル国 形モンゴル人[語]の

☐ **monotheistic religion** 一神教

☐ **mood** 名気分, 機嫌, 雰囲気, 憂うつ

☐ **more than** ～以上

☐ **moreover** 副その上, さらに

☐ **Morse code** モールス信号

☐ **mortality rate** 死亡率

☐ **mostly** 副主として, 多くは, ほとんど

☐ **motel** 名モーテル

☐ **mountaintop** 名山頂

☐ **move to** ～に引っ越す

☐ **movement** 名①動き, 運動 ②《-s》行動 ③引っ越し ④変動

☐ **Muhammad** 名ムハンマド《ア

A
B
C
D
E
F
G
H
I
J
K
L
M
N
O
P
Q
R
S
T
U
V
W
X
Y
Z

ラブの指導者・イスラム教の預言者,
570?–632》

- [ ] **multiple** 形 複合的な, 多様な
- [ ] **murder** 名 人殺し, 殺害, 殺人事件
  動 殺す
- [ ] **murderer** 名 殺人犯
- [ ] **museum** 名 博物館, 美術館
- [ ] **musician** 名 音楽家
- [ ] **Muslim** 名 イスラム教徒, ムスリ
  ム 形 イスラム教［文明］の
- [ ] **mutilate** 動 (手足などを)切断す
  る
- [ ] **My God.** おや, まあ
- [ ] **mystery** 名 神秘, 不可思議

N

- [ ] **naked** 形 裸の
- [ ] **narrow** 形 狭い
- [ ] **NASA** 略 アメリカ航空宇宙局
  《 National Aeronautics and Space
  Administration の略》
- [ ] **nation** 名 国, 国家,《the –》国民
- [ ] **national** 形 国家［国民］の, 全国の
- [ ] **navy** 名 海軍, 海軍力
- [ ] **nearby** 形 近くの, 間近の 副 近く
  で, 間近で
- [ ] **nearly** 副 ほとんど
- [ ] **necessary** 形 必要な, 必然の 名
  《-s》必要品, 必需品
- [ ] **need to do** ～する必要がある
- [ ] **needless** 形 不必要な
- [ ] **needy** 形 貧乏な, お金に困って, す
  がるような
- [ ] **neither** 副《否定文に続いて》～も
  …しない
- [ ] **Nellie Connally** ネリー・コナリ
  ー《テキサス州の政治家, ジョン・コ
  ナリーの夫人, 1919–2006》
- [ ] **Nelly** 名 ネリー《ボートの名》

- [ ] **network** 名 回路, 網状組織, ネッ
  トワーク
- [ ] **network-based** 形 ネットワー
  ク基盤の
- [ ] **neural** 形 神経の, 神経系の
- [ ] **neural network** ニューラルネ
  ットワーク《「入力を線形変換する処
  理単位」がネットワーク状に結合した
  人工知能の数理モデル》
- [ ] **neuron** 名 ニューロン, 神経単位
- [ ] **New Guinea** ニュー・ギニア
- [ ] **New Jersey** ニュージャージー州
- [ ] **New World** 《the –》アメリカ大
  陸, 新世界
- [ ] **New York** ニューヨーク《米国の
  都市；州》
- [ ] **New York City** ニューヨーク市
- [ ] **Newfoundland** 名 ニューファ
  ンドランド島《カナダ東海岸に位置す
  る島》
- [ ] **news** 名 報道, ニュース, 便り, 知
  らせ
- [ ] **newspaper** 名 新聞（紙）
- [ ] **next in line** 列の順番が次
- [ ] **Nicholas II, Tsar** ニコライ2世
  《ロマノフ朝第14代にして最後のロ
  シア皇帝, 在位 1894–1917》
- [ ] **9/11** アメリカ同時多発テロ事件
  《2001年9月11日にアメリカ合衆国
  で発生した, 航空機を使った4つのテ
  ロ事件の総称》
- [ ] **1917 revolution** ロシア革命《史
  上初の社会主義国家樹立につながっ
  た1917年にロシア帝国で起きた2度
  の革命》
- [ ] **no longer** もはや～でない［～し
  ない］
- [ ] **no one** 誰も［一人も］～ない
- [ ] **Nobel Peace Prize** ノーベル平
  和賞
- [ ] **noble** 形 貴族の
- [ ] **nobody** 代 誰も［1人も］～ない

- [ ] **nod** 動 うなずいて～を示す
- [ ] **noise** 名 騒音, 騒ぎ, 物音
- [ ] **non-Christian** 名 非キリスト教徒 形 非キリスト教徒の
- [ ] **normal** 形 普通の, 平均の, 標準的な
- [ ] **normally** 副 普通は, 通常は
- [ ] **Northern Ireland** 北アイルランド
- [ ] **not** 熟 not matter 問題にならない not only ～ but (also) …～だけでなく…もまた not yet まだ～してない not ～ but … ～ではなくて… whether or not ～かどうか
- [ ] **not ～ but** ～ではなくて…
- [ ] **not matter** 問題にならない
- [ ] **not yet** まだ～してない
- [ ] **note** 名 ①メモ, 覚え書き ②注釈 ③注意, 注目 ④手形 動 ①書き留める ②注意[注目]する
- [ ] **notice** 名 公告 動 気づく
- [ ] **now-famous** 形 今では有名となった
- [ ] **nowhere** 副 どこにも～ない
- [ ] **nuclear** 形 核の, 原子力の
- [ ] **nuclear power plant** 原子力発電所
- [ ] **nuclear reactor** 原子炉
- [ ] **nuclear-power accident** 原子力事故
- [ ] **number** 熟 large number of 多数の～, 多くの～
- [ ] **numerous** 形 多数の
- [ ] **nurse** 名 乳母
- [ ] **nurture** 動 養育する, 育てる 名 養育

O

- [ ] **object** 名 物

- [ ] **observe** 動 ①観察[観測]する, 監視[注視]する ②気づく ③守る, 遵守する
- [ ] **obstacle** 名 障害(物), じゃま(な物)
- [ ] **occur** 動 (事が)起こる, 生じる
- [ ] **odd job** 臨時仕事, 雑務
- [ ] **of course** もちろん, 当然
- [ ] **of the time** 当時の, 当節の
- [ ] **officer** 名 役人, 公務員, 警察官 police officer 警察官
- [ ] **officially** 副 公式に, 職務上, 正式に
- [ ] **Olga** 名 オリガ(・ニコラエヴナ)《ニコライ2世第一皇女, 1895-1918》
- [ ] **on the other hand** 一方, 他方では
- [ ] **onboard** 形 (乗り物に)搭載された
- [ ] **once** 熟 at once すぐに, 同時に
- [ ] **one** 熟 at one time ある時には, かつては loved one 最愛の人 one of ～の1つ[人]
- [ ] **one-third** 名 3分の1(の)
- [ ] **oneself** 熟 by oneself 一人で, 自分だけで, 独力で for oneself 独力で, 自分のために
- [ ] **only** 熟 not only ～ but (also) …～だけでなく…もまた
- [ ] **open wagon** 無蓋車
- [ ] **opening** 名 開いた所, 穴
- [ ] **open-top car** オープンカー
- [ ] **operate** 動 ①(機械などが)動く, 運転する, 管理する, 操業する ②作用する ③手術する
- [ ] **operation** 名 作戦, 軍事行動
- [ ] **opponent** 形 敵対する, 反対する 名 競争相手, 敵, 反対者
- [ ] **opportunity** 名 好機, 適当な時期[状況]
- [ ] **opposition** 名 ①反対 ②野党

- ☐ **oppression** 名圧迫, 抑圧, 重荷
- ☐ **option** 名選択 (の余地), 選択可能物, 選択権
- ☐ **order** 熟in order for ~ to … ~が…するために in order to ~するために, ~しようと
- ☐ **ordinary** 形①普通の, 通常の ②並の, 平凡な
- ☐ **organ** 名(体の) 器官
- ☐ **origin** 名起源, 出自
- ☐ **originate** 動始まる, 始める, 起こす, 生じる
- ☐ **originator** 名創始者, 開祖
- ☐ **Osama bin Laden** ウサマ・ビン・ラディン《サウジアラビア出身のイスラム過激派テロリスト, 1957–2011》
- ☐ **other** 熟each other お互いに in other words すなわち, 言い換えれば on the other hand 一方, 他方では
- ☐ **otherwise** 副さもないと, そうでなければ
- ☐ **Our American Cousin** 『われらのアメリカのいとこ』《イギリス貴族遺産相続にアメリカ人の甥がからむ喜劇》
- ☐ **out** 熟break out 発生する, (戦争が) 勃発する carry out [計画を] 実行する drive someone out (人) を追い払う out of ~から外へ
- ☐ **outbreak** 名勃発, 発生
- ☐ **outcome** 名結果, 結末
- ☐ **outlet** 名放送 [テレビ・ラジオ] 局
- ☐ **over** 熟all over ~中で, ~の至る所で all over the world 世界中に over and over 何度も繰り返して take over 引き継ぐ, 支配する, 乗っ取る
- ☐ **over and over** 何度も繰り返して
- ☐ **overcome** 動勝つ, 打ち勝つ, 克服する be overcome with ~に圧倒

される, ~にやられる
- ☐ **overthrew** 動overthrow (ひっくり返す) の過去
- ☐ **overthrow** 動①ひっくり返す②転覆する, 廃止する
- ☐ **overthrown** 動overthrow (ひっくり返す) の過去分詞
- ☐ **oxygen** 名酸素

P

- ☐ **pacific** 形①平和な, 穏やかな ②《P-》太平洋の 名《the P-》太平洋
- ☐ **Pacific Islands** 太平洋諸島
- ☐ **package** 名包み, 小包
- ☐ **paid** 動pay (払う) の過去, 過去分詞
- ☐ **painful** 形痛い, 苦しい, 痛ましい
- ☐ **pair** 名(2つから成る) 一対, 一組, ペア
- ☐ **pajama** 名《通例-s》パジャマ
- ☐ **Pakistan** 名パキスタン《国名》
- ☐ **palace** 名宮殿, 大邸宅
- ☐ **Palestinian** 形パレスチナの, パレスチナ人の
- ☐ **pandemic** 名パンデミック《複数の国や全世界など, 広域でまん延する深刻な感染症の大流行》
- ☐ **panicked** 形うろたえた
- ☐ **paparazzi** 名パパラッチ《(有名人を追い回す) 追っかけカメラマン》
- ☐ **paradigm shift** パラダイムシフト《その時代や分野において前提とされていた認識や思想, 社会全体の価値観などが劇的に変化すること》
- ☐ **parent** 名《-s》両親
- ☐ **Paris** 名パリ《フランスの首都》
- ☐ **Parkland Memorial Hospital** パークランド・メモリアル病院
- ☐ **participate** 動参加する, 加わる

□ **particular** 形 ①特別の ②詳細な 名 事項, 細部, 《-s》詳細 **in particular** 特に, とりわけ

□ **pass down** (次の世代に)伝える

□ **passenger** 名 乗客, 旅客

□ **past** 形 過去の, この前の 名 過去(の出来事) 前 《時間・場所》〜を過ぎて, 〜を越して 副 通り越して, 過ぎて

□ **path** 名 ①(踏まれてできた)小道, 歩道 ②進路, 通路

□ **pattern** 名 ①柄, 型, 模様 ②手本, 模範 動 ①手本にする ②模様をつける

□ **pause** 動 休止する

□ **pay** 動 ①支払う, 払う, 報いる, 償う ②割に合う, ペイする 名 給料, 報い

□ **payment** 名 支払い, 払い込み

□ **peasant** 名 農民, 小作人

□ **Pence** 名 《Mike –》マイク・ペンス《アメリカ合衆国第48代副大統領(2017–2021), 1959–》

□ **Pennsylvania** 名 ペンシルベニア州

□ **Pentagon** 名 ペンタゴン《アメリカ合衆国の国防総省の本部庁舎》

□ **per** 前 〜につき, 〜ごとに

□ **perform** 動 (任務などを)行う, 果たす, 実行する

□ **perhaps** 副 たぶん, ことによると

□ **period** 名 ①期, 期間, 時代 ②ピリオド, 終わり

□ **permissive** 形 寛大な, 許す

□ **persecute** 動 迫害する, 虐待する

□ **persecution** 名 迫害, 虐待

□ **personal** 形 ①個人の, 私的な ②本人自らの

□ **personality** 名 人格, 個性

□ **perspective** 名 ①遠近法 ②観点 ③見通し 形 遠近法の

□ **Peter and Paul Cathedral** 首座使徒ペトル・パウェル大聖堂《ロシア・サンクトペテルブルクのペトロパヴロフスク要塞にあるロシア正教会の聖堂》

□ **Phoenix Islands** フェニックス諸島《太平洋にあるキリバス領の諸島》

□ **photo** 名 写真

□ **photographer** 名 写真家, カメラマン

□ **pick up** 拾い上げる, 車で迎えに行く, 習得する, 再開する, 回復する

□ **picture** 熟 take a picture 写真を撮る

□ **pillar** 名 ①柱, 支柱, 支え ②根幹

□ **pilot** 名 パイロット, 操縦士

□ **pioneer** 名 開拓者, 先駆者

□ **Pittsburgh** 名 ピッツバーグ《ペンシルベニア州》

□ **pity** 名 哀れみ, 同情, 残念なこと **take pity on** 〜に同情を示す, 〜を哀れむ

□ **place** 熟 take place 行われる, 起こる

□ **plague** 名 ①疫病, 伝染病, ペスト ②天災

□ **plan to do** 〜するつもりである

□ **plastic bag** ビニール袋

□ **plaza** 名 広場

□ **poet** 名 詩人, 歌人

□ **point** 熟 at this point 現在のところ, この時点で **point of view** 考え方, 視点 **point out** 指し示す, 指摘する, 目を向ける, 目を向けさせる

□ **Poitiers** 名 ポワティエ《フランスの地名》

□ **pole** 名 柱

□ **police officer** 警察官

□ **policy** 名 政策, 方針

□ **political** 形 政治の

□ **politically** 副 政治上, 政治的に

□ **politician** 名 政治家, 政略家

A
B
C
D
E
F
G
H
I
J
K
L
M
N
O
P
Q
R
S
T
U
V
W
X
Y
Z

□ **politics** 图政治(学), 政策
international politics 国際政治

□ **polo** 图ポロ《馬に乗って行う球技》

□ **pomegranate** 图《植物》ザクロ

□ **pool** 图プール

□ **pope** ①《the P-》ローマ教皇 ②教祖

□ **popular among** 《be－》～の間で人気がある

□ **population** 图人口, 住民(数)

□ **port** 图港, 港町

□ **position** 图①位置, 場所, 姿勢 ②地位, 身分, 職 ③立場, 状況

□ **possibility** 图可能性, 見込み, 将来性

□ **possible** 形①可能な ②ありうる, 起こりうる

□ **possibly** 副あるいは, たぶん

□ **poverty** 图貧乏, 貧困, 欠乏, 不足

□ **power plant** 発電所

□ **power surge** 電力サージ

□ **pray for** ～のために祈る

□ **preacher** 图(プロテスタントの)説教師, 牧師

□ **precious** 形大事な

□ **predict** 動予測[予想]する

□ **predictable** 形予測できる, 意外性のない

□ **prefer** 動(～のほうを)好む, (～のほうが)よいと思う

□ **prejudice** 图偏見, 先入観

□ **pre-school teacher** 幼稚園[保育園]の教師

□ **preserve** 動保存[保護]する, 保つ

□ **president** 图①大統領 ②社長, 学長, 頭取

□ **president-elect** 图《米》〔就任前の〕次期大統領 形《米》大統領に選ばれた, 次期大統領の

□ **presidential** 形大統領の

□ **Presidential Box** 大統領用ボックス席

□ **pressure** 图プレッシャー, 圧力, 圧縮, 重荷 **be under pressure to** ～する必要に迫られている

□ **prevent** 動①妨げる, じゃまする ②予防する, 守る, 《－～ from …》～が…できない[しない]ようにする

□ **pride** 图誇り, 自慢, 自尊心 動《－oneself》誇る, 自慢する

□ **prime minister** 総理大臣, 首相

□ **prince** 图王子, プリンス

□ **Prince Charles** チャールズ(プリンス・オブ・ウェールズ)《エリザベス2世第一王子, 現国王チャールズ3世(2022–), 1948–》

□ **princess** 图王女

□ **Princess Diana** ウェールズ公妃ダイアナ《ウェールズ公チャールズの最初の妃, 1961–1997》

□ **prior** 形(時間・順序が)前の, (～に)優先する, (～より)重要な

□ **Pripyat** 图プリピャチ《ウクライナの北部にある市。チェルノブイリ原子力発電所事故によって住民が避難したため現在は無人》

□ **prison** 图刑務所, 監獄

□ **prisoner** 图囚人, 捕虜

□ **private** 形私的な, 個人の

□ **privilege** 图特権

□ **privileged** 形特権を持つ

□ **procedure** 图手順, 手続き

□ **procession** 图行進, 行列
funeral procession 葬列

□ **product** 图①製品, 産物 ②成果, 結果

□ **production** 图製造, 生産

□ **profitable** 形利益になる, 有益な

□ **promised** 形約束した

□ **promote** 動促進する, 昇進[昇級]させる

□ **proof** 图①証拠, 証明 ②試し, 吟

味 ③《-s》校正刷り, ゲラ

□ **proper** 形 ①適した, 適切な, 正しい ②固有の

□ **property** 名 ①財産, 所有物[地] ②性質, 属性

□ **prosperity** 名 繁栄, 繁盛, 成功

□ **prostitute** 名 売春婦

□ **protector** 名 ①保護者 ②保護するもの, プロテクター

□ **protest** 動 ①主張[断言]する ②抗議する, 反対する 名 抗議(書), 不服

□ **Protestant** 名 プロテスタント

□ **prove** 動 ①証明する ②(～である ことが)わかる (～と)なる

□ **provide** 動 ①供給する, 用意する, (～に)備える ②規定する

□ **public** 名 一般の人々, 大衆 形 公の, 公開の be made public 公になる public statement 公式声明

□ **publish** 動 ①発表[公表]する ②出版[発行]する

□ **publisher** 名 出版社, 発行者

□ **punish** 動 罰する, ひどい目にあわせる

□ **punishment** 名 ①罰, 処罰 ②罰を受けること

□ **pursuit** 名 追跡, 追求

□ **put ~ into ...** ～を…の状態にする, ～を…に突っ込む

□ **put on** 熟 ①～を身につける, 着る ②～を…の上に置く

□ **put on trial for** 《be –》～のかどで裁判に掛けられる

□ **put out** (明かり・火を)消す

□ **put to death** 《be –》処刑される

□ **puzzle** 動 迷わせる, 当惑する[させる]

□ **Pyrenees Mountains** ピレネー山脈《フランス・スペイン・アンドラ公国の3か国にまたがる山脈》

Q

□ **quack remedy** いんちき療法

□ **quarantena** 名 〈イタリア語〉40日《検疫を意味する名詞 quarantine の語源》

□ **quarantine** 名 ①〔病原体に感染した可能性のある人の〕隔離 ②〔船などの〕検疫 動 ①〔病原体に感染した可能性のある人を〕隔離する ②〔船などを〕検疫する

□ **queen** 名 女王, 王妃

□ **quickly** 副 敏速に, 急いで

□ **quietly** 副 ①静かに ②平穏に, 控えめに

□ **quit** 動 やめる, 辞職する, 中止する

R

□ **racial** 形 人種の, 民族の

□ **racism** 名 人種差別(主義)

□ **radiation** 名 放射(能), 放射線

□ **radical** 形 急進的な, 過激な 名 急進主義者, 過激派

□ **radicalize** 動 ①〔政治的に～を〕急進的にする ②〔～を〕根本的に改革する

□ **radio** 名 ①ラジオ ②無線電話[電報]

□ **radioactive** 形 放射能の, 放射性の radioactive material/matter 放射性物質

□ **rage** 名 激怒, 猛威, 熱狂

□ **railroad** 名 鉄道, 路線

□ **raise** 動 ①上げる, 高める ②起こす

□ **Ralph David Abernathy** ラルフ・デヴィッド・アバナシー《アメリカ合衆国の牧師, 公民権運動指導者, 1926–1990》

□ **rampage** 名 暴れ回ること, 大暴れ, 暴力事件

□ **rang** 動 ring (鳴る)の過去

A
B
C
D
E
F
G
H
I
J
K
L
M
N
O
P
Q
R
S
T
U
V
W
X
Y
Z

- □ **range** 名 列, 連なり, 範囲 動 ①並ぶ, 並べる ②およぶ
- □ **ranger** 名 警備員, 監視人, レインジャー
- □ **ransom** 名 身代金, 賠償金
- □ **rapidly** 副 速く, 急速, すばやく, 迅速に
- □ **rat** 名 ①ネズミ (鼠) ②裏切り者
- □ **rate** 名 ①割合, 率 ②相場, 料金 **mortality rate** 死亡率
- □ **rather** 副 ①むしろ, かえって ②かなり, いくぶん, やや ③それどころか逆に **rather than** ～よりむしろ
- □ **react** 動 反応する, 対処する
- □ **reactor** 名 原子炉
- □ **reader** 名 読者
- □ **ready for** 《be –》準備が整って, ～に期待する
- □ **ready to** 《be –》すぐに [いつでも] ～できる, ～する構えで
- □ **reality** 名 現実, 実在, 真実 (性)
- □ **realize** 動 理解する, 実現する
- □ **reason for** ～の理由
- □ **recent** 形 近ごろの, 近代の
- □ **reception** 名 受付
- □ **recognize** 動 認める, 認識 [承認] する
- □ **recommend** 動 勧告する, 忠告する
- □ **record** 名 ①記録, 登録, 履歴 ②(音楽などの) レコード 動 記録 [登録] する
- □ **Record Plant Studios** レコード・プラント・スタジオ《録音スタジオ》
- □ **recover** 動 ①取り戻す, ばん回する ②回復する
- □ **recovery** 名 回復, 復旧, 立ち直り
- □ **Red Army** 赤軍《1918年から1946年にかけてロシアおよびソビエト連邦に存在した軍隊》

- □ **Red Cross** 赤十字社
- □ **reduce** 動 ①減じる ②しいて～させる, (～の) 状態にする
- □ **reexamine** 動 再検査する, もう一度調べる, 見直す
- □ **reformation** 名 ①矯正, 改心, 改良, 改善 ②《R-》宗教改革
- □ **regardless** 形 無頓着な, 注意しない 副 それにもかかわらず, それでも
- □ **region** 名 ①地方, 地域 ②範囲
- □ **regulation** 名 規則, 規定, 規制
- □ **reign** 名 ①治世 ②君臨, 支配 動 君臨する, 支配する
- □ **reject** 動 拒絶する, 断る
- □ **relation** 名 親戚
- □ **relationship** 名 関係, 関連
- □ **relax** 動 くつろぐ
- □ **release** 動 解き放す
- □ **religion** 名 宗教
- □ **religious** 形 宗教の
- □ **remain** 動 依然として～のままである
- □ **remind** 動 思い出させる, 気づかせる
- □ **removal** 名 除去, 移動
- □ **remove** 動 取り去る, 除去する
- □ **Renaissance** 名 ①《the –》ルネッサンス, 文芸復興 (運動) ②ルネッサンス様式 ③《時にr-》(芸術・学問の) 復興
- □ **repair** 名 修理, 修繕
- □ **repeat** 動 繰り返す
- □ **repeated** 動 repeat (繰り返す) の過去, 過去分詞 形 繰り返された, 度重なる
- □ **replace** 動 取り替える, 差し替える
- □ **reportedly** 副 伝えられるところによれば
- □ **reporter** 名 レポーター, 報告者, 記者

□ **represent** 動 ①表現する ②意味する ③代表する

□ **representative** 名 代表(者)

□ **Republican Party** 《the – 》〈米〉共和党

□ **reputation** 名 評判, 名声, 世評

□ **require** 動 ①必要とする, 要する ②命じる, 請求する

□ **research** 名 調査, 研究

□ **resent** 不快に思う, 憤慨する

□ **reserve** 動 ①とっておく, 備えておく ②予約する

□ **resident** 名 居住者, 在住者

□ **resource** 名 ①資源, 財産 ②手段, 力量 **financial resource** 金融資産, 財源

□ **respect** 名 尊敬, 尊重 動 尊敬[尊重]する

□ **respond** 動 答える, 返答[応答]する

□ **response** 名 応答, 反応, 返答

□ **responsible** 形 責任のある, 信頼できる, 確実な

□ **restricted** 動 restrict (制限する) の過去, 過去分詞 形 制限された, 限られた

□ **result** 名 結果, 成り行き **as a result** その結果(として) **as a result of** ～の結果(として) 動 (結果として)起こる, 生じる, 結局～になる

□ **retake** 動 〔～を〕取り戻す

□ **return to** ～に戻る, ～に帰る

□ **revenge** 名 復讐

□ **revival** 名 復活, 再生, リバイバル

□ **revolt** 動 そむく, 反乱を起こす

□ **revolution** 名 ①革命, 変革 ②回転, 旋回 **Industrial Revolution** 産業革命

□ **revolutionize** 動 大変革[革命]をもたらす, 根本的に変える

□ **rid** 動 取り除く **get rid of** ～を取り除く

□ **rig** 動 〔価格・取引・入札・選挙などを〕不正操作する

□ **right** 熟 **civil rights** 公民権

□ **rightful** 形 正当な, 当然の

□ **rightward** 形 右方向の, 右側の

□ **riot** 名 暴動, 騒動

□ **rioter** 名 暴徒, 暴民

□ **ripper** 名 引き裂く人

□ **RMS** 略 英国郵便汽船《Royal Mail Ship の略》

□ **RMS Titanic** タイタニック《20世紀初頭に建造された豪華客船》

□ **rob** 動 奪う, 金品を盗む, 襲う

□ **robbery** 名 泥棒, 強盗

□ **rock'n'roll** 名 ロックンロール

□ **role** 名 ①(劇などの)役 ②役割, 任務

□ **Rolling Stone** 『ローリング・ストーン』《雑誌名》

□ **Roman Catholic Church** 《the – 》ローマカトリック教会

□ **Roman Catholicism** ローマカトリック教

□ **Roman Empire** 《the – 》帝政ローマ, ローマ帝国

□ **Romanov Family** ロマノフ家《ロシア帝国を統治していた皇室》

□ **romantic** 形 ロマンチックな, 空想的な

□ **Romeo and Juliet** ロミオとジュリエット

□ **Roosevelt Hospital** 聖路加ルーズベルト病院

□ **root** 名 ①根, 根元 ②根源, 原因 ③《-s》先祖, ルーツ **take root** 根づく, 定着する 動 根づかせる, 根づく **rooted in** 《be – 》～に根ざしている

□ **roughly** 副 おおよそ, 概略的に, 大ざっぱに

□ **round** 名 (銃・武器などの)一発分

151

の弾

- □ **route** 名道, 道筋, 進路, 回路
- □ **Roy Thornton** ロイ・ソーントン 《ボニー・パーカーの夫, 高校時代の同級生, 1908–1937》
- □ **royal** 形王の, 女王の, 国立の
- □ **royal family** 王室
- □ **royalty** 名特権階級, 王位
- □ **ruin** 名破滅, 滅亡, 廃墟 **in ruins** 廃墟となって, 荒廃して
- □ **rule** 動〔独裁的・専制的に国などを〕統治〔支配〕する
- □ **rule over** 治める, 統御する
- □ **ruler** 名支配者
- □ **rumor** 名うわさ
- □ **run away** 走り去る, 逃げ出す
- □ **run from** ～から逃れる
- □ **run low** 残り少なくなる
- □ **run out of** ～が不足する, ～を使い果たす
- □ **run through** 走り抜ける
- □ **runoff election** 決選投票
- □ **rural** 形田舎の, 地方の
- □ **rush** 動突進する, せき立てる
- □ **Russia** 名ロシア《国名》
- □ **Russian** 名ロシア(人・語)の 名①ロシア人 ②ロシア語
- □ **Russian Civil War** ロシア内戦 《1917年から1922年にかけて旧ロシア帝国領で争われた内戦》
- □ **Russian Revolution** ロシア革命《史上初の社会主義国家樹立につながった1917年にロシア帝国で起きた2度の革命》
- □ **rye** 名ライ麦

S

- □ **sadden** 動～を悲しませる
- □ **sadness** 名悲しみ, 悲哀

- □ **safe** 副無事に
- □ **safely** 副安全に, 間違いなく
- □ **safety** 名安全, 無事, 確実
- □ **sail** 名帆走, 航海 **set sail** 出帆〔出航〕する 動帆走する, 航海する
- □ **sale** 名販売, 取引, 大売り出し
- □ **same** 熟 **the same ～ as**〔**that**〕 …―と同じ(ような) ～
- □ **Samoa** 名サモア諸島《南太平洋上に位置する島々》
- □ **sank** 動 sink (沈む) の過去
- □ **Sarah** 名セーラ(・マッコーコデール)《ダイアナの姉, 1955–》
- □ **SARS-CoV-2** 名新型コロナウイルスのウイルス名
- □ **saving** 名①節約 ②《-s》貯金 ③救助 **life savings** 老後の蓄え, ためてきたお金
- □ **schoolbook** 名教科書
- □ **scientific** 形科学の, 科学的な
- □ **scream** 名金切り声, 絶叫
- □ **Sean** 名ショーン・レノン《ジョン・レノンの次男, 1975–》
- □ **search** 動捜し求める, 調べる 名捜査, 探索, 調査
- □ **searching** 名捜査, 探索, 調査
- □ **second-most** 形2番目に最も～な
- □ **secret** 形秘密の, 隠れた 名秘密
- □ **secretary of state** 国務長官
- □ **secretly** 副秘密に, 内緒で
- □ **sect** 名派閥, 学派, 宗派
- □ **secure** 形①安全な ②しっかりした, 保証された 動①安全にする ②確保する, 手に入れる
- □ **security** 名①安全(性), 安心 ②担保, 抵当,《-ties》有価証券
- □ **see ～ as ...** ～を…と考える
- □ **see if** ～かどうかを確かめる
- □ **seem** 動(～に)見える, (～のように)思われる **seem to be** ～である

Word List

ように思われる

□ **seemingly** 副見たところでは, 外見は

□ **self-driving** 形〔車などが〕自動運転の

□ **senate** 名①《the S-》(米・仏などの)上院 ②《the -》(古代ローマの)元老院 ③(大学などの)評議会

□ **send away** 追い払う, 送り出す

□ **sense** 名意味

□ **sentence** 名①文 ②判決, 宣告 動判決を下す, 宣告する

□ **separate** 動①分ける, 分かれる, 隔てる ②別れる, 別れさせる

□ **coparation** 名①分離(点), 離脱, 分類, 別離

□ **serial** 形連続している, 連載の **serial killer** 連続殺人犯 **serial number** シリアルナンバー, 通し番号

□ **series** 名一続き, 連続, シリーズ

□ **serious** 形①まじめな, 真剣な ②重大な, 深刻な, (病気などが)重い

□ **seriously** 副①真剣に, まじめに ②重大に

□ **serve** 動①仕える, 奉仕する ②(役目を)果たす, 務める, 役に立つ

□ **service** 名①勤務, 業務 ②公益事業 ③点検, 修理 ④奉仕, 貢献 動保守点検する, (点検)修理をする

□ **service module** 機械船《アポロ宇宙船の一部。アポロ宇宙船は司令船, 機械船の2つで構成され, 機械船は推進用のロケットエンジンと姿勢制御用の小ロケットエンジンおよびその燃料, さらに宇宙滞在中に必要な酸素, 水, バッテリーなどの消耗品などを搭載している》

□ **set free** (人)を解放する, 釈放される, 自由の身になる

□ **set pattern** 決まったパターン

□ **set sail** 出帆[出航]する

□ **set up** 配置する, セットする, 据え付ける

□ **severely** 副厳しく, 簡素に

□ **shadow** 名影, 暗がり

□ **shake** 動①振る, 揺れる, 揺さぶる, 震える ②動揺させる 名①振ること ②ミルクセーキ

□ **shed** 動①(涙・血を)流す ②(服・皮・殻などを)脱ぐすてる, 脱皮[脱毛, 落葉]する ③捨てる, 解雇する

□ **shift** 動移す, 変える, 転嫁する 名①変化, 移動 ②交替, (交代制の)勤務(時間), シフト

□ **shock** 熟go into shock ショック状態に陥る in a state of shock 狂乱状態で

□ **shook** 動shake (振る)の過去

□ **shooting** 名射撃, 発砲

□ **shortly** 副まもなく, すぐに

□ **shoulder** 名肩

□ **shown** 動show (見せる)の過去分詞

□ **shut** 動①閉まる, 閉める, 閉じる ②たたむ ③閉じ込める ④shutの過去, 過去分詞

□ **Sicily** 名シチリア[シシリー・シシリア]島《イタリア半島の最南端の西に位置する島》

□ **sick and tired of** 《be -》〜にうんざりしている

□ **sickness** 名病気

□ **side** 名側, 横, そば

□ **sight** 熟at first sight 一目で

□ **signal** 名信号, 合図

□ **significance** 名重要(性), 意味, 深刻さ

□ **silence** 名沈黙, 無言, 静寂

□ **silent** 形静かな, 音を立てない

□ **Silicon Valley** シリコンバレー《米国カリフォルニア州の工業集積地域, 半導体製造企業が多い》

□ **similar** 形同じような, 類似した, 相似の **similar to** 《be -》〜に似て

A B C D E F G H I J K L M N O P Q R S T U V W X Y Z

いる

- □ **similarly** 副 同様に, 類似して, 同じように
- □ **simply** 副 単に, ただ
- □ **simulation** 名 ①シミュレーション ②ふりをすること
- □ **single** 形 ①たった1つの ②1人用の, それぞれの ③独身の ④片道の
- □ **sink** 動 沈む, 沈める
- □ **sinking** 名 沈没
- □ **sit up** 起き上がる, 上半身を起こす
- □ **situation** 名 ①場所, 位置 ②状況, 境遇, 立場
- □ **sixteenth** 名 第16番目(の人[物]), 16日 形 第16番目の
- □ **slavery** 名 奴隷制度, 奴隷状態
- □ **slight** 形 ①わずかな ②ほっそりして ③とるに足らない
- □ **slogan** 名 スローガン, モットー
- □ **slowly** 副 遅く, ゆっくり
- □ **small-time** 形 取るに足りない, 軽犯罪の, 三流の
- □ **smoke** 名 煙 cloud of smoke もうもうとした煙
- □ **smoothly** 副 滑らかに, 流ちょうに
- □ **so** 熟 so many 非常に多くの so that ～するために, それで, ～できるように so ～ as to … …するほど～で so ～ that … 非常に～なので…
- □ **social** 形 ①社会の, 社会的な ②社交的な, 愛想のよい
- □ **social climbing** 立身出世(すること)
- □ **socialize** 動 ①社会化する ②社会に適合させる ③社交的にする
- □ **society** 名 社会, 世間
- □ **soil** 名 土, 土地
- □ **soldier** 名 兵士, 兵卒
- □ **solid** 形 ①固体[固形]の ②頑丈な ③信頼できる

- □ **solution** 名 ①分解, 溶解 ②解決, 解明, 回答
- □ **solve** 動 解く, 解決する
- □ **some time** いつか, そのうち
- □ **somebody** 代 誰か, ある人
- □ **somehow** 副 ①どうにかこうにか, ともかく, 何とかして ②どういうわけか
- □ **someone** 代 ある人, 誰か drive someone out (人)を追い払う
- □ **something** 代 ①ある物, 何か ②いくぶん, 多少 something is wrong with ～はどこか具合が悪い
- □ **sometimes** 副 時々, 時たま
- □ **soon as** 《as-》～するとすぐ, ～するや否や
- □ **sort of** ～のようなもの, 一種の～
- □ **sound like** ～のように聞こえる
- □ **source** 名 源, 原因, もと
- □ **South America** 南アメリカ
- □ **Southampton** 名 サウサンプトン港《イギリス》
- □ **southeast** 名 南東(部)
- □ **southern** 形 南の, 南向きの, 南からの
- □ **Soviet** 形 (旧ソビエト連邦の)会議の
- □ **spaceship** 名 宇宙船
- □ **Spain** 名 スペイン《国名》
- □ **Spanish** 形 スペイン(人・語)の 名 ①スペイン人 ②スペイン語
- □ **Spanish Flu** スペイン風邪《1918年に発生した最悪のインフルエンザ》
- □ **speaking** 熟 generally speaking 一般的に言えば speaking of ～について言えば
- □ **special agent** 特別捜査官
- □ **specialize** 動 専門にする, 専攻する, 特別にする
- □ **specially** 副 特別に
- □ **sped** 動 speed (急ぐ)の過去, 過去

分詞

- □ **speech** 熟 make a speech 演説をする

- □ **spine** 名 背骨, 脊柱

- □ **spiritual** 形 精神の, 精神的な, 霊的な

- □ **split** 動 裂く, 裂ける, 割る, 割れる, 分裂させる〔する〕 名 ①裂くこと, 割れること ②裂け目, 割れ目

- □ **spot** 名 地点, 場所, 立場 on the spot その場で, ただちに

- □ **spring up** (急に) 生じる

- □ **Springfield** 名 スプリングフィールド《イリノイ州の州都》

- □ **sprung** 動 spring (跳ねる) の過去・過去分詞

- □ **square** 名 正方形, 四角い広場, (市外の) 一区画 形 正方形の, 四角な, 直角な, 角ばった

- □ **St. Joseph's Hospital** 聖ジョセフ病院

- □ **St. Petersburg** サンクトペテルブルク《ロシア, レニングラード州の州都》

- □ **stab** 動 (突き) 刺す

- □ **stage** 名 ①舞台 ②段階 動 〔イベントを〕主催する, 計画的に実施する

- □ **stance** 名 ①〔人や動物の立つ〕構え, 姿勢 ②〔物事に対する〕心構え, 立場, 態度

- □ **stand by** 熟 そばに立つ, 傍観する, 待機する

- □ **start to do** ～し始める

- □ **state** 名 ①あり様, 状態 ②国家, (アメリカなどの) 州 ③階層, 地位 動 述べる, 表明する

- □ **statement** 名 声明, 述べること

- □ **status** 名 ①(社会的な) 地位, 身分, 立場 ②状態

- □ **steadily** 副 しっかりと

- □ **steal** 動 盗む

- □ **steer** 動 舵をとる, 操縦する

- □ **Steve Jobs** スティーブ・ジョブズ《アップル社の共同設立者の一人, 1955-2011》

- □ **stimulate** 動 ①刺激する ②促す, 活性化させる ③元気づける

- □ **stole** 動 steal (盗む) の過去

- □ **stomach** 名 胃, 腹

- □ **stop by** 途中で立ち寄る, ちょっと訪ねる

- □ **stir** 動 動かす, かき回す stir up 荒立てる, 引き起こす 名 動き, かき回すこと

- □ **strain** 動 緊張させる, ぴんと張る

- □ **stranger** 名 見知らぬ人, 他人

- □ **strategize** 動 〔～を〕戦略化する

- □ **strengthening** 名 強化

- □ **stretch** 動 引き伸ばす, 広がる, 広げる 名 ①伸ばす〔伸びる〕こと, 広がり ②ストレッチ (運動)

- □ **strongly** 副 強く, 頑丈に, 猛烈に, 熱心に

- □ **struck** 動 strike (打つ) の過去, 過去分詞

- □ **struggle** 動 もがく, 奮闘する 名 もがき, 奮闘

- □ **stubborn** 形 頑固な, 強情な

- □ **studio** 名 スタジオ

- □ **subcontractor** 名 協力会社, 下請け業者

- □ **subsequent** 形 次の, 続いて起きる, その結果生じた

- □ **succeed** 動 ①成功する ②(～の) 跡を継ぐ

- □ **successful** 形 成功した, うまくいった

- □ **successfully** 副 首尾よく, うまく

- □ **such a** そのような

- □ **such as** たとえば～, ～のような

- □ **sudden** 形 突然の, 急な

- □ **suffering** 動 suffer (受ける) の現在分詞 名 苦痛, 苦しみ, 苦難

□ **suffocation** 名 窒息

□ **suggest** 動 ①提案する ②示唆する

□ **suicide** 名 自殺

□ **supercomputer** 名 スーパーコンピュータ

□ **superpower** 名 超大国, 強国, 異常な力

□ **support** 動 ①支える, 支持する ②養う, 援助する

□ **supporter** 名 後援者, 支持者

□ **suppose** 動 《be -d to ～》～することになっている, ～するものである

□ **suppression** 名 鎮圧, 抑制, 隠蔽

□ **sure** 熟 make sure 確かめる, 確認する, 必ずする

□ **surge** 名 急上昇

□ **surpass** 動 勝る, しのぐ

□ **surprise attack** 奇襲(攻撃)

□ **surround** 動 囲む, 包囲する

□ **surrounding** 形 周囲の

□ **survival** 名 生き残ること, 生存者, 残存物

□ **survive** 動 生き残る, 存続する

□ **suspect** 名 容疑者, 注意人物

□ **Sweden** 名 スウェーデン《国名》

□ **swell** 動 ①ふくらむ, ふくらませる ②増加する, 増やす

□ **swelling** 名 腫れ(物), こぶ

□ **swimming pool** スイミング[水泳]プール

□ **switch** 名 スイッチ 動 ①スイッチを入れる[切る] ②切り替える, 切り替わる

□ **symbol** 名 シンボル, 象徴

T

□ **take** 熟 It takes someone ～ to …(人)が…するのに～(時間など)がかかる take a picture 写真を撮る take advantage of ～を利用する, ～につけ込む take away ①連れ去る ②取り上げる, 奪い去る ③取り除く take control of ～を制御[管理]する, 支配する take good care of ～を大事に扱う, 大切にする take off (衣服を)脱ぐ, 取り去る take on (仕事などを)引き受ける take out of ～から連れ出す take over 引き継ぐ, 支配する, 乗っ取る take pity on ～に同情を示す, ～を哀れむ take place 行われる, 起こる take root 根づく, 定着する take someone away (人)を連れ出す take the form of ～となって現れる take ～ to …～を…に連れて行く

□ **Take My Hand, Precious Lord** テイク・マイ・ハンド・プレシャス・ロード(慕いまつる主なるイエスよ)《ゴスペル》

□ **Taliban** 名 タリバーン《パキスタンとアフガニスタンで活動するイスラム主義運動》

□ **tank** 名 タンク, 戦車

□ **tape** 名 テープ, 接着テープ

□ **target** 名 標的, 目的物, 対象

□ **Tatiana** 名 タチアナ(・ニコラエヴナ)《ニコライ2世第二皇女, 1897–1918》

□ **tax** 名 税

□ **technologically** 副 技術的に

□ **technology** 名 テクノロジー, 科学技術

□ **telegraph** 名 電報, 電信 動 電報を打つ

□ **television** 名 テレビ

□ **temperature** 名 温度, 体温

□ **tendency** 名 傾向, 風潮, 性癖

□ **Tennessee** 名 テネシー州

□ **tension** 名 緊張(関係), ぴんと張ること

□ **term** 名 ①期間, 期限 ②語, 用語 ③《-s》条件 ④《-s》関係, 仲 in

左余白インデックス: A B C D E F G H I J K L M N O P Q R **S** T U V W X Y Z terms of ～の点から

- **terrain** 图 地形, 地勢
- **terribly** 副 ひどく
- **territorial** 形 領土の, 領土に関する, 土地の
- **territory** 图 ①領土 ②（広い）地域, 範囲, 領域
- **terror** 图 ①恐怖 ②テロ（行為） War on Terror テロとの戦い《アメリカ同時多発テロをうけて, 当時のブッシュ大統領が掲げたスローガン》
- **terrorism** 图 テロ行為, 暴力行為
- **terrorist** 图 テロリスト
- **terrorist activity** テロ活動
- **terrorize** 動 こわがらせる, 脅かす, テロ行為を行う
- **Tesla** 图 テスラ《米国の電動輸送機器・クリーンエネルギー関連企業》
- **Texas** 图 テキサス州
- **Texas Ranger** テキサス・レンジャー《テキサス州警備隊の隊員》
- **Texas Schoolbook Depository** テキサス教科書倉庫
- **text** 图 本文, 原本, テキスト, 教科書
- **than** 熟 more than ～以上
- **that** 熟 after that その後 at that time その時 so that ～するために, それで, ～できるように so ～ that … 非常に～なので…
- **theatre** 图 劇場
- **theory** 图 理論, 学説
- **there** 熟 get there そこに到着する, 目的を達成する, 成功する
- **therefore** 副 したがって, それゆえ, その結果
- **thick** 形 厚い
- **thin** 形 薄い
- **think of** ～のことを考える, ～を思いつく, 考え出す
- **thinker** 图 思想家, 考える人
- **thinking** 動 think（思う）の現在分

詞 图 考えること, 思考 形 思考力のある, 考える

- **this** 熟 at this これを見て, そこで（すぐに）at this point 現在のところ this way このように
- **Thomas Andrews** トーマス・アンドリューズ《アイルランド出身の造船家, タイタニック号の設計を担当, 1873–1912》
- **those** 熟 in those days あのころは, 当時は those who ～する人々
- **though** 接 ①～にもかかわらず, ～だが ②たとえ～でも even though ～にもかかわらず 副 しかし
- **thought of as** 《be –》～（である）と考えられる
- **thread** 图 糸, 糸のように細いもの 動 糸を通す
- **threat** 图 おどし, 脅迫
- **threaten** 動 脅かす, おびやかす, 脅迫する
- **three dimensions** 三次元
- **Three Mile Island Nuclear Power Plant** スリーマイル島原子力発電所《ペンシルベニア州》
- **throat** 图 のど, 気管
- **throne** 图 王座, 王権
- **throughout** 前 ①～中, ～を通じて ②～のいたるところに
- **tight** 形 堅い, きつい, ぴんと張った 副 堅く, しっかりと
- **time** 熟 at a time 一度に, 続けざまに at one time ある時には, かつては at that time その時 at the time そのころ, 当時は by the time ～する時までに by this time この時までに, もうすでに each time ～するたびに every time ～するときはいつも for a time しばらく, 一時の間 of the time 当時の, 当節の some time いつか, そのうち
- **tip** 图 先端, 頂点
- **tired** 形 ①疲れた, くたびれた ②あきた, うんざりした be sick and

tired of ～にうんざりしている

☐ **Titanic** 名 タイタニック号《20世紀初頭に建造された豪華客船》

☐ **to begin with** はじめに, まず第一に

☐ **tolerant** 形 寛容な, 寛大な

☐ **tolerate** 動 我慢する, 寛大に扱う

☐ **toll** 〔事故や災害の〕犠牲者, 損害, 死傷者数 **death toll** 死亡者数

☐ **tore** 動 tear (裂く) の過去

☐ **total** 形 総計の, 全体の, 完全な 名 全体, 合計

☐ **Tours** 名 トゥール《フランスの地名》

☐ **trace** 名 ①跡 ②（事件などの）こん跡 動 たどる, さかのぼって調べる

☐ **track** 動 追跡する

☐ **trade** 名 取引, 貿易, 商業

☐ **traditional** 形 伝統的な

☐ **traditionally** 副 伝統的に, 元々は

☐ **tragedy** 名 悲劇, 惨劇

☐ **tragic** 形 悲劇の, 痛ましい

☐ **training** 名 トレーニング, 訓練

☐ **transform** 動 ①変形［変化］する, 変える ②変換する

☐ **treat** 動 ①扱う ②治療する ③おごる 名 ①おごり, もてなし, ごちそう ②楽しみ

☐ **treatment** 名 取り扱い, 待遇

☐ **trial** 名 裁判 **be put on trial for ～** のかどで裁判に掛けられる

☐ **truck** 名 トラック, 運搬車

☐ **truly** 副 ①全く, 本当に, 真に ②心から, 誠実に

☐ **Trump** 名《Donald ～》ドナルド・トランプ《アメリカ合衆国第45代大統領（2017–21）, 1946–》

☐ **truth** 名 ①真理, 事実, 本当 ②誠実, 忠実さ

☐ **tsar** 名 (旧ロシア) 皇帝

☐ **Tsarina Alexandra** 旧ロシア皇后アレクサンドラ（・フョードロヴナ）《ニコライ2世第二皇女, 1897–1918》

☐ **tsarist** 名 皇帝の

☐ **turmoil** 名 動揺, 騒動, 混乱

☐ **turn** 熟 **in turn** 順番に, 立ち代わって **turn around** 振り向く, 向きを変える, 方向転換する **turn off** ～を止める, （照明などを）消す

U

☐ **Ukraine** 名 ウクライナ《国名》

☐ **ultimately** 副 最終的に, 結局, 究極的に

☐ **Umayyad** 名 ウマイヤ朝《イスラム史上最初の世襲イスラム王朝, 661–750》

☐ **unable** 形《be – to ～》～することができない

☐ **underlie** 動 基礎となる, 下に横たわる

☐ **undermine** 動 ①（～の）下を掘る ②徐々に弱める, ひそかに傷つける

☐ **underpin** 動 ①～を下から支える, 下支えする ②〔主張などを〕支持する, 根拠を与える

☐ **unearth** 動 〔～を〕掘り出す, 発掘する

☐ **unfairly** 副 不当に

☐ **unfit** 形 向いていない, 適さない

☐ **unhappy** 形 不運な, 不幸な

☐ **United States** 名 アメリカ合衆国《国名》

☐ **universe** 名《the – /the U-》宇宙, 全世界

☐ **university** 名 (総合) 大学

☐ **unknown** 形 知られていない, 不明の

☐ **unless** 接 もし～でなければ, ～しなければ

Word List

- □ **unlikely** 形 ありそうもない，考えられない

- □ **unpleasant** 形 不愉快な，気にさわる，いやな，不快な

- □ **unpopular** 形 人気がない，はやらない

- □ **unprecedented** 形 前例のない，かつてない，前代未聞の

- □ **unrest** 名 不安，心配，動揺

- □ **unsanitary** 形 非[不]衛生的な

- □ **untrue** 形 真実でない，事実に反する

- □ **unusually** 副 異常に，珍しく

- □ **unveil** 動 ベールを取る，明らかにする

- □ **up** 熟 spring up（急に）生じる stir up 荒立てる，引き起こす up to ～まで，～に至るまで，～に匹敵して

- □ **up to** ～まで，～に至るまで，～に匹敵して

- □ **upon** 前 ①《場所・接触》～（の上）に ②《日・時》～に ③《関係・従事》～に関して，～について，～して 副 前へ，続けて

- □ **upper** 形 上の，上位の，北方の

- □ **upset** 動 気を悪くさせる，（心・神経など）をかき乱す

- □ **upstairs** 副 2階へ[に]，階上へ

- □ **U.S.** 略 《the –》（アメリカ）合衆国（= United States）

- □ **used** 動 ①use（使う）の過去，過去分詞 ②《– to》よく～したものだ，以前は～であった 形 ①慣れている，《get [become] – to》～に慣れてくる ②使われた，中古の

- □ **useless** 形 役に立たない，無益な

- □ **usual** 形 通常の，いつもの，平常の，普通の as usual いつものように，相変わらず go about business as usual 普段どおりに仕事をする

- □ **utilize** 動 利用する，活用する

V

- □ **vaccination** 名 ワクチン接種，予防接種

- □ **valley** 名 谷，谷間

- □ **valuable** 形 貴重な，価値のある，役に立つ

- □ **value** 名 価値，値打ち，価格 動 評価する，値をつける，大切にする

- □ **variety** 名 ①変化，多様性，寄せ集め ②種類

- □ **various** 形 変化に富んだ，さまざまの，たくさんの

- □ **vast** 形 広大な，巨大な，ばく大な

- □ **vehicle** 名 乗り物，車，車両

- □ **Venice** 名 ヴェネチア，ヴェニス《イタリアの都市》

- □ **venture** 動 思い切って～する，危険にさらす 名 冒険（的事業），危険

- □ **Versailles** 名 ベルサイユ《フランス北中部の都市》

- □ **version** 名 ①バージョン，版，翻訳 ②意見，説明，解釈

- □ **vice president** 副大統領

- □ **vicious** 形 悪意のある，意地の悪い，扱いにくい

- □ **victim** 名 犠牲者，被害者

- □ **Vienna** 名 ウィーン《オーストリアの首都》

- □ **view** 熟 point of view 考え方，視点

- □ **vineyard** 名 （ワイン醸造用の）ブドウ園

- □ **violence** 名 ①暴力，乱暴 ②激しさ

- □ **Virginia** 名 バージニア州

- □ **virus** 名 ウイルス

- □ **vision** 名 ①視力 ②先見，洞察力

- □ **vote** 名 投票（権），票決 動 投票する，投票して決める

- □ **voter** 名 投票者

- □ **voyage** 名 航海，航行

W

☐ **wagon** 图荷馬車, ワゴン（車）

☐ **wait for** ～を待つ

☐ **Wales** 图ウェールズ《英国南西部の地方》

☐ **walk on** 歩き続ける

☐ **walk up** 歩み寄る, 歩いて上る

☐ **Wall Street** 〈米〉ウォール街, 米国金融市場《ニューヨークの金融街》

☐ **Wallis Simpson** ウォリス・シンプソン《ウィンザー公爵（元イギリス国王エドワード8世）夫人, 1896–1986》

☐ **wander** 動さまよう, 放浪する

☐ **war** 图Civil War アメリカ南北戦争《1861–65》 Russian Civil War ロシア内戦《1917年から1922年にかけて旧ロシア帝国領で争われた内戦》

☐ **War on Terror** テロとの戦い《アメリカ同時多発テロをうけて, 当時のブッシュ大統領が掲げたスローガン》

☐ **warn** 動警告する, 用心させる

☐ **warning light** 警告灯

☐ **Warren Commission** ウォーレン委員会《ケネディ大統領暗殺事件を検証するために設置された調査委員会》

☐ **wary** 形用心深い, 慎重な

☐ **Washington, D.C.** ワシントンD.C.

☐ **water-tight** 形防水の, 水密の

☐ **wave** 動（手などを振って）合図する

☐ **way** 图go a long way 大いに役立つ on one's way to ～に行く途中で this way このように way to ～する方法

☐ **wealth** 图富, 財産

☐ **wealthy** 形裕福な, 金持ちの

☐ **wed** 動結婚させる, 結婚する

☐ **weep** 動しくしく泣く, 嘆き悲しむ

☐ **weight** 图重さ

☐ **well** 熟as well その上, 同様に as well as ～と同様に do well 成績が良い, 成功する

☐ **well-known** 形よく知られた, 有名な

☐ **well-loved** 形心から愛されている

☐ **western** ①西の, 西側の ②《W-》西洋の

☐ **Western Europe** 西欧, 西ヨーロッパ

☐ **Western Heights Cemetery** ウエスタンハイツ墓地

☐ **Westminster Abbey** ウェストミンスター寺院

☐ **westward** 图西方 形西へ, 西向きの

☐ **wheel** 图①輪, 車輪《the –》ハンドル ②旋回 動①回転する［させる］②～を押す

☐ **whether** 接～かどうか, ～かまたは…, ～であろうとなかろうと whether or not ～かどうか

☐ **which** 熟of which ～の中で

☐ **while** 熟for a while しばらくの間, 少しの間

☐ **White Army** 白軍《1917年以降のロシア革命期における反革命側の軍隊の総称》

☐ **White House** アメリカ大統領官邸, ホワイト・ハウス

☐ **White Star Line** ホワイト・スター・ライン社《イギリスの海運企業》

☐ **Whitechapel** 图ホワイトチャペル《ロンドン市街地の地区名》

☐ **who** 熟anybody who ～する人は誰でも those who ～する人々

☐ **whoever** 代～する人は誰でも, 誰が～しようとも

☐ **whole** 形全体の, すべての, 完全な, 満～, 丸～

☐ **whom** 代①誰を［に］②《関係代

名詞》〜するところの人, そしてその
人を

□ **wide** 形幅の広い, 広範囲の, 幅が
〜ある 副広く, 大きく開いて

□ **widely** 副広く, 広範囲にわたって

□ **William** 名ウィリアム (ケンブリ
ッジ公)《ウェールズ公チャールズと
ダイアナ妃の長男, 現皇太子, 1982-》

□ **willingly** 副喜んで, 快く

□ **Wilmer Stultz** ウィルマー・スタ
ールズ《飛行士, 1900-1929》

□ **windowsill** 名窓の下枠

□ **wipe** 動〜をふく, ぬぐう, ふきと
る 名ふくこと

□ **wire** 名①針金 電線 ②電信 動電
報を打つ, 配線をする

□ **with** 熟 along with 〜と一緒に
begin with 〜で始まる to begin
with はじめに, まず第一に

□ **within** 副①〜の中[内]に, 〜の内
部に ②〜以内で, 〜を越えないで

□ **witness** 動目撃する

□ **wives** 名 wife (妻) の複数

□ **wonder** 動①不思議に思う, (〜
に) 驚く ②(〜かしらと) 思う 名驚
き (の念), 不思議なもの

□ **wooden** 形木製の, 木でできた

□ **word** 熟 in other words すなわち,
言い換えれば

□ **work of** 〜の仕事

□ **work on** 〜で働く, 〜に取り組む,
〜を説得する, 〜に効く

□ **worker** 名仕事をする人, 労働者

□ **workhouse** 名救貧院

□ **world** 熟 all over the world 世界
中に

□ **World Trade Center** 世界貿易
センター《かつてニューヨーク市マン
ハッタン区のローワー・マンハッタ
ンに位置していた商業センター》

□ **World War I** 第一次世界大戦
《1914-1918》

□ **worldwide** 形世界的な, 世界中
に広まった, 世界規模の 副世界中
[で], 世界的に

□ **worried** 形心配そうな, 不安げな

□ **worse** 形いっそう悪い, より劣っ
た, よりひどい get worse 悪化する

□ **worst** 形《the-》最も悪い, いち
ばんひどい

□ **would like to** 〜したいと思う

□ **wound** 名傷

□ **writer** 名書き手, 作家

□ **wrong** 熟 be wrong with (〜に
とって) よくない, 〜が故障している
something is wrong with 〜はどこ
か具合が悪い

Y

□ **years** 熟 for years 何年も for 〜
years 〜年間, 〜年にわたって

□ **Yekaterinburg** 名エカテリンブ
ルク《ロシア連邦, スヴェルドロフス
ク州の州都》

□ **yet** 熟 and yet それなのに, それに
もかかわらず not yet まだ〜してな
い

□ **yield** 動①生じる, 産出する ②譲
る, 明け渡す 名①産出(物, 高), 収
穫(量) ②利回り, 利益

□ **Yoko Ono** オノ・ヨーコ《日本
生まれのアメリカの芸術家, 音楽家,
1933-》

161

English Conversational Ability Test
国際英語会話能力検定

● **E-CATとは…**
英語が話せるようになるための
テストです。インターネット
ベースで、30分であなたの発
話力をチェックします。

www.ecatexam.com

● **iTEP®とは…**
世界各国の企業、政府機関、アメリカの大学
300校以上が、英語能力判定テストとして採用。
オンラインによる90分のテストで文法、リー
ディング、リスニング、ライティング、スピー
キングの5技能をスコア化。iTEP®は、留学、就
職、海外赴任などに必要な、世界に通用する英
語力を総合的に評価する画期的なテストです。

www.itepexamjapan.com

ラダーシリーズ
A History of Western Tragedies and Accidents
世界の重大事件［増補改訂版］

2023年7月6日　第1刷発行

著　者　　ニーナ・ウェグナー

発行者　　浦　晋亮

発行所　　**IBCパブリッシング株式会社**
　　　　　〒162-0804 東京都新宿区中里町29番3号
　　　　　菱秀神楽坂ビル
　　　　　Tel. 03-3513-4511　Fax. 03-3513-4512
　　　　　www.ibcpub.co.jp

印刷　株式会社シナノパブリッシングプレス
装丁　伊藤　理恵
カバーイラスト　iStock.com/S_Bachstroem

落丁本・乱丁本は、小社宛にお送りください。送料小社負担にてお取り替えいたします。本書の無断複写（コピー）は著作権法上での例外を除き禁じられています。

Printed in Japan
ISBN978-4-7946-0766-9